CAN MAN BE MODIFIED?

CAN MAN BE MODIFIED?

by
JEAN ROSTAND

Translated from the French
by
JONATHAN GRIFFIN

New York
BASIC BOOKS, INC.
1959

Printed in the United States of America

Library of Congress Catalog Card Number: 59–8370

CONTENTS

I

VICTORIES AND HOPES OF BIOLOGY

TO SAY THAT OUR WORLD IS CONSTANTLY expanding is a commonplace. It is expanding in every sense, in every field, and in every direction. Almost all the discoveries made in the last few years have resulted in pushing frontiers further away, in making origins more remote. The universe is vaster than it was thought to be, the earth more ancient, man older . . . And the world is expanding not only in time and in space: it expands every time a new idea appears, every time men acquire a new power. There is the expansion of mathematics through the inclusion of the transfinite; the expansion of the field of mind through the exploration of the subconscious; the expansion of technology through cybernetics and nuclear physics; and the expansion of every discipline through the deepening of complexity, which is indeed, as Teilhard de Chardin has put it, a sort of 'third infinite', containing abysses in no way inferior to those of greatness and smallness.

As for biology, or the science of life, it looks as if we have at last finally staked out its dimensional limits, which run from a ten thousandth of a millimetre (viruses) to thirty-five metres (the blue whale). It is thanks to the relatively recent invention of the electron microscope, a product of wave mechanics, that we have succeeded in penetrating into the field of the viruses, and we have reason to believe that with them we are reaching a real limit. It is impossible to imagine, as Pascal did, that within the body of one of the mites of our universe there lodges another universe peopled with other mites, for the phenomenon of vitality cer-. tainly stops at a certain level of size, not far from that of the larger chemical molecules.

None the less, biology is still growing continuously as an experimental science, as a 'victorious and practical' science, the dispenser of fresh powers. This is the aspect of its expansion that will concern us here. We will start by enumerating some of its more recent advances, in virtue of which it really is a kind of positive magic – taking the word magic in the honourable sense in which the great Francis Bacon used it when he called by that name 'that great liberty and latitude of operation which dependeth upon the knowledge of forms.'

★

The operations performed daily by the biologist are, for 'liberty and latitude', hard to surpass.

The egg of an animal – a sea-urchin's, a frog's or a rabbit's – is normally formed by the conjunction of two reproductive cells, the maternal cell or ovum, and the paternal cell or spermatozoon. We now have the power to replace one of the constituent cells – the paternal one – by chemical agents of very different kinds.

People are even beginning to be rather *blasé* about this fatherless generation, or artificial parthenogenesis; but let us not forget that the first scientists to obtain it – half a century ago already – could not believe their own eyes. 'When I announced the successful chemical fertilisation of sea-urchins,' says Jacques Loeb, 'the almost unanimous opinion was that I had been the victim of an illusion, and at first I myself was afraid I had been mistaken.' In the grave pages of the *Annales des Sciences naturelles* the French zoologist Viguier indulged in irony at the expense of so-called 'chemical citizens, the sons of Madame Sea-Urchin and Monsieur Chloride of Magnesium'. As for Eugène Bataillon, when he saw the first fatherless tadpoles fluttering about in his test tubes, he was, as he himself admits, obsessed by the fear that some frog sperm might have polluted the water from his taps . . .

We have now digested all this – so much so that not long ago, at the Institut de France, the permanent secretary of the Académie des Sciences referred quite calmly to the prospect of solitary generation for human beings.

It is now a regular thing for perfectly constituted living creatures to be born from a virgin egg without any help from a male, on condition that within this egg there has been produced a doubling of the chromosomes – in other words, a doubling of those cellular particles which play a preponderant part in heredity. The results are living creatures that carry a *double charge of heredity from the mother's side*, instead of carrying, as do their fellows with two parents, one charge of maternal heredity and one of paternal.

But, it may be said, if we can at will double the maternal chromosomes in a virgin egg, could not the same thing be done just as well in an egg that had been fertilised and so provided with the father's chromosomes? This experiment has in fact been carried out on salamanders, on frogs and perhaps even on rabbits and pigs. Its result is to obtain creatures of a somewhat baroque composition from the point of view of heredity, since they possess three stocks of chromosomes instead of two, and, having only one paternal stock as against two maternal, must be considered as *their mother's children twice over and their father's only once.*

Instead of increasing heredity from the mother's side, we can simply do away with it, by extracting from the egg or destroying in it the maternal chromosomes: it then develops with the father's chromosomes alone. In this way we shall have caused an 'androgenesis', a sort of pendant to parthenogenesis in that it gives birth to creatures with a purely, or more or less purely, paternal heredity.

But biology does not confine itself to these minor and already classic variants: it is embroidering still further on the inexhaustible theme of generation. In 1955 it added to its resources a truly original and rather unexpected method of reproduction, which it owes to the fine experiments of the American biologists Briggs and King.

By means of a fine pipette, the nucleus – that is to say chromosomes – is removed from a frog's egg. Then another nucleus is introduced, taken from one of the many cells that compose a frog's embryo. The egg that has been completed afresh in this way develops regularly and yields a normal creature, with a chromosome make-up strictly similar to that of the donor embryo, so that it will be a sort of 'retarded twin' of the latter, rather than a real descendant.

The main interest of this experiment is that it shows that any of the numerous nuclei of the embyro can set in motion the development of the egg. It proves that any of these nuclei possesses the genetic value of a germinal nucleus. The researches, which are still going on, have up to now [1956] been applied only to more or less advanced embryos; but it may turn out that analogous results could be obtained with nuclei taken from a larva or even from an adult animal . . . And, to push the thing to its extreme, it is possible to imagine that all the cells of the body – skin cells, muscle cells, gland cells – contain what is needed to make an egg develop. Every speck of flesh would then be charged with seminal virtue. In each element of a living creature there would reside the principle of the whole creature.

In a book written a long time ago I timidly suggested this overwhelming possibility of conferring physical immortality upon a human being by exploiting the potential immortality assured to him by tissue culture: 'If a biologist', I said, 'takes a tiny fragment of tissue from the freshly dead body, he could make from it one of those cultures which we know to be immortal, and there is no absolute reason why we should not imagine the perfected science of the future as capable of re-making from such a culture the complete person, strictly identical to the one who had furnished its principle.'

Well, that forecast is now in process of being realised since the experiments of Briggs and King. It may be added that this new technique of generation from the nucleus of a body cell would in theory enable us to create as many identical individuals as might be desired. A living creature would be printed in hun-dreds, in thousands of copies, *all of them real twins*. This would, in short, be *human propagation by cuttings*, capable of assuring the indefinite reproduction of the same in-dividual – of a great man, for example!

In discussing fatherless generation we saw that the female had an advantage over the male, in that she produces the large cell which serves as germ and is self-sufficient. But the male regains a certain advantage in the fact that his tiny seminal cells offer a considerable resistance to cold: whence the possibility of putting them into cold storage for an indefinite period.

I showed in 1946 that a frog's seminal cells, when in contact with diluted glycerine, can endure prolonged congealment without perishing. This observation was followed up by the important work of Parkes's London team, which has established that a cock's or bull's semen treated with glycerine can support extremely low temperatures – of the order of 80° below zero (carbonic snow), and even more – without losing the power to fertilise.

This technique has now been extended to the human species. Bunge and Sherman, two progressive doctors in Iowa, have caused three births by means of a semen thus vitrified for several months in a medium containing glycerine. The children, so far, are perfectly normal.

If semen endures a condition of vitrifying congealment for several months, could it perhaps do so for several years, several centuries? If so, we can, by only a slight extension, envisage the possibility of human reproduction a very long time after death. We are already accustomed to the idea that living semen can travel (by aeroplane, in a thermos flask), can cross the oceans and so operate the germinal mingling of two individuals that are continents apart. Now, like space, time is ceasing to be an obstacle to genetic mingling. Here, after telegenesis, comes palaeogenesis. One cannot help thinking of Diderot's prophecy, in *Le Rêve de d'Alembert*: 'A warm room with the floor covered with little pots, and on each of these pots a label: soldiers, magistrates, philosophers, poets, potted courtesans, potted kings . . .' The only difference is that, instead of a warm room, we must provide a cold one.

On the basis of this data supplied by the science of our time, a writer of science fiction might imagine, some millions of years hence, when the earth, dead and buried under ice, is no more than a gigantic refrigerator, some traveller from another planet arriving in a 'flying saucer', and finding in the ruins of one of our laboratories a vitrified sample of human semen, thanks to which the ancient chromosomes of *homo sapiens* might come into play once more, in alliance with those of a female from Mars or from Venus.

In any case, the spermatozoon is certainly the only form in which the human race could conceivably resist the freezing of the globe.

*

If further illustrations of the magical side of biology are required, there are enough and to spare.

The fertilised egg can be taken from the female and placed in the matrix of another female of the same species, which will then, when the moment comes, give birth to creatures that will not be its own descendants. The experiment has been made on female rabbits, on cows and on mares.

By dividing up a germ cell with a well-aimed stroke of the scalpel we can multiply the organic person making several individuals – all of them alike, all of them twins – arise from a germ cell which would have produced only one. It was in this way that the great biologist Etienne Wolff, with the assistance of Hubert Lutz, produced the birth of *quintuplet ducklings*, so achieving experimentally what nature does spontaneously in the case of man, when real twins or Siamese twins are formed.

There is also the fascinating – and somewhat disquieting – field of *sex transformations*: an operation that, to the biologist, has become a game, a trick, ever since he had at his disposal, in the pure and crystallised state, those powerful drugs, the sexual hormones.

The hormones – of which everyone has heard, if only through advertisements for medicines – are truly magical substances when they are employed with knowledge and in sufficient quantities. In the sexual hormones we have masculinity and femininity powers, and since every organism contains the characteristics of both sexes potentially, we need only administer to it one or the other hormone to make it exhibit one or the other group of characteristics. In this way there is nothing easier than to realise regularly among the fauna of the laboratories the strange adventure of Robert Cowell, the English airman who turned into Roberta!

Not only can we confer upon an animal of masculine type the whole outward aspect of the feminine type, forcing for instance a golden pheasant to exchange his radiant plumage for the hen pheasant's dull dress, but we can also, provided that we intervene at an early enough age, alter the evolution of the sexual organs themselves. If the hormone is used during the embryonic development, intersexual individuals are obtained – hermaphrodites, ambiguous creatures in which male and female attributes are found side by side or intermingling: males with a vaginal opening, females afflicted with a prostate.

If the hormone operates even earlier, right at the beginning of development, it upsets and reverses completely the processes of sexual differentiation: a male creature will be born from an egg that was originally determined as female; a female creature from an egg originally determined as male.

B

And, what is more, these false males that started as females and these false females that started as males are such good imitations that they can be made to reproduce according to their artificial sex. Using salamanders and toads, false males have been coupled with true females and false females with true males, and from these unions descendants have been obtained that were the issue of two mothers or two fathers.

This neat experiment has been carried out by the American biologist Humphrey and by the French biologist Gallien. As might have been expected, the proportion of the sexes among the products of homosexual unions is modified. From the coupling of two male salamanders, only male young can be produced. And, while the coupling of two female salamanders makes it possible to obtain both sexes, it none the less produces an excessive proportion of females, among which are to be found abnormal ones, *hyperfemales* as it were, which, even if coupled with authentic males, can only have daughters . . . These females incapable of giving birth to sons do not exist in nature; they are real creations of the laboratory.

The sexual hormones enable us to do other things besides juggle with sexual structure. The female hormone, folliculin, brings on heat in rats; the male hormone makes a young cock crow when he is scarcely out of his shell.

Another hormone – prolactin, which comes from the pituitary gland and is strictly the hormone of maternity – forces chickens to brood when they do not desire to remain on the nest, and makes toads move towards a pond when they do not wish to bathe. If a mother hippopotamus begins to eat one of her young, it is enough to rub her with an ointment containing pro-lactin to re-establish better feelings in her and prevent fresh infanticides.

By using other hormones, also produced by the pituitary gland, we can start a precocious puberty in mice, make fish and frogs lay eggs or eject their milt, or cause multiple pregnancy in animals like cows or ewes in which single pregnancy is normal. Through the use of other pituitary hormones rats or dogs are made to grow beyond the normal size of the species. With the thyroid hormone, which causes an early metamorphosis in tadpoles, dwarf frogs scarcely as big as flies are obtained, while in certain insects, by means of the hormone of the *corpora allata*, the number of moults or changes of skin is increased, allowing the animal to prolong its period of growth and to attain a length double the standard length.

Leaving out of this brief review of the exploits of present day biology the artificial production of monsters by means of X-rays or chemical substances, we will confine ourselves to mentioning, in connection with grafting or transplantation, the pretty experiment which consists in grafting the eye of a salamander (*salamandrida*) on to the body of a newt (*triton*). The foreign eye begins to function again, it perceives, it sees, but since the salamander has less sharpness of vision than the newt, what has been created by this means is a composite animal, a chimera, that sees slightly better than a salamander, though rather less well than a newt.

Animals belonging to the higher groups, such as birds and mammals, do not, as a rule, take well to the grafting of organs, for their organic individuality constitutes an obstacle that is usually impassable. It is none the less possible, in certain cases, to make young organs taken from embryos or still-births start functioning again. For instance, May and Huignard quote the case of a cretinous child who, through the implanting of some embryonic thyroid gland, put on height and rose in his class at school.

Let us conclude this list by referring to the culture of separate organs, begun in 1936 by Carrel and Lindbergh. It consists in making isolated organs – a heart, a lung, a womb, a thyroid gland – go on living outside the body. For example, Petters and Massart kept a cow's udder alive, so that in the test tube it produced milk, and was milked from the teats.

Etienne Wolff recently gave a further impulse to this method by the culture of *embryonic organs* of chickens or mice, so bringing about 'growth by spare parts'. He removed sexual glands when they were still at the stage of undifferentiated suggestions, shin bones when they were mere tiny wands of cartilege and fragments of skin, or eyes when they were still minute translucent vesicles attached to the brain. And in the small saltcellar which served as the receptacle for the culture, he watched the sexual gland turn into an ovary or a testicle, he watched the shin bone lengthen and become curved and mould its extremities as though in articulation with a phantom thigh bone and foot, he watched the skin bristle with budding feathers as it took on its characteristic look of 'goose flesh', and he watched the globe of the eye swell and acquire colour.

He could even, by adding to the nutrient solution a few drops of a solution of one of the sexual hormones, change at will, while he watched, the sex of the gland which he was culturing.

Researches of this kind may contain the rudiments of *ectogenesis*, or test tube pregnancy, which Aldous Huxley promised us in his well known novel, *Brave New World*.

Finally, let us not forget that the biologist's powers are not exercised merely upon the individual organism. They extend to the race, to descendants, to the species, since by means of penetrative radiations or of certain poisons such as mustard gas we can bring into being animals or plants with abnormal characteristics that are transmissible to their descendants. In a word, we can produce *artificial mutations* and cause new races of living creatures to appear on earth. It is indeed, be it said in passing, upon these experiments with artificial mutation – the first of which were due to Muller in 1927 – that the great fear felt by biologists in face of the liberation of atomic energy is based, and based very solidly: they know, in fact, that a fresh cause of mutations has been introduced by this into the world; and, knowing also that almost all mutations – if not all – tend to deteriorate the species, they find themselves forced to conclude that, as from now, science has declared war on the hereditary patrimony of mankind.

★

Such is an extremely summary review of what might be called the feats of biology. Is there any need to add that this rather spectacular, rather sensational aspect, on which we have insisted for the sake of making the magical power of our science felt, is not at all what the investigator seeks? Not for a second does the biologist set out to show off or aim at virtuoso exploits; if he does find himself engaged in such strange exercises, it is because they are his only means of subjecting to analysis the phenomenon with which animated nature presents him. Researches of this kind have enabled men to take to pieces, and in part to explain, manifestations of heredity, sex and growth.

The upshot of all this is that, from now on, we possess the means of acting upon life. Our 'liberty and latitude of operation' is due to our having penetrated into the secrets of nature. To our having laid hands on some of its mainsprings. To our beginning to know at what point to strike – which are the sensitive spots. To our having stolen from life some of its recipes.

But it now behoves us to question ourselves seriously about the value of our conquests, about the bearing and significance of this expansion of human power which results from biology. To be sure, our first impulse is one of enthusiasm, of marvelling and of limitless hope . . . Have not the biologists the right to a little conceit, when they add up what they have achieved in the space of a mere half century? Would they not be justified in believing that to them all things will become possible, simply by going on deepening the trenches already dug and continuing along the lines of researches already marked out?

Since science already replaces the seminal cell in its work of fecundation, why should it not tomorrow create life? Since it creates races and fresh lines of descent, why should it not tomorrow create species and genera – why should it not achieve mastery of organic evolution and, in particular, of human evolution?

But this is where we must remind ourselves that our successes, amazing as they are, leave the formidable riddles of life itself almost intact. The three cardinal problems of biology – the problem of how a living creature grows, the problem of how species evolve, the problem of how life originated – have been scarcely touched by the scientists. We have no more than a very vague idea of the way in which a complex organism can be contained in a germ; we have hardly any idea of the way in which the organic metamorphoses that must have gone to produce the human species from some original virus may have been accomplished in the course of ages, and we have not the slightest idea of the way in which the first lives were born.

And so, after having stressed how extraordinary, how prodigious biology is, it remains for us now to note how much superficiality and speciousness there is, none the less, in this magic of ours. After the moment of pride comes the time for modesty. Let us contrive to reduce our prentice triumphs to their proper proportion and to tone down our transports of pygmy exultation.

The general public is prone to believe that to have caused the birth of animals without a father is the same as to have half created life, and looks forward to the time when science, by replacing both the generative cells, will have wholly created life. But in fact it has created nothing, for it has replaced the father merely as agent of stimulation, not as father. Similarly, when we make an embryo arise at a point in the germ cell where it ought not to have appeared, we have not created this embryo at all – all we have done is to realise the conditions for its genesis. Similarly again, when we invert the sex of an organism, we have not created sexual characteristics, we have merely favoured their manifestation.

'Really we create nothing,' as that great scientist, Eugène Bataillon, used to say again and again towards the end of his life – and, coming from the inventor of traumatic parthenogenesis, this expression of humility could not fail to be impressive. And again he used to say: 'We merely plagiarise nature, and our plagiarism has not the perfection of the original . . . When we succeed, it is because, on some imperceptibly small point, our logic has turned out to be in conformity with a logic that goes prodigiously beyond us . . . The prentice sorcerer may, here and there, complicate the straight path with a detour or a short cut, but never beyond the power of sovereign law to bring him back to the normal way.'[1] Those are strong, fine words, on which we can never meditate too much.

For it is indeed true that all the biologist's power is incapable of creating a cell, or a nucleus, or a chromosome, or a gene . . . We alter relationships or quantities,

[1] See his admirable little book, *Enquête sur la génération*, Editions Sedes, 1955.

we modify the rhythms, we bring this or that factor into action earlier or later, or we suppress it, or we invert the order of events, or we introduce in this place something that should only operate somewhere else, or we bring into massive action a substance that normally intervenes only in very small quantities: in short, we play tricks upon the egg or the embryo. And certainly, by teasing them in this way, we can amuse ourselves and gain instruction to the end of time. We combine, we transpose, we interpose, we interlard, but at every stage we are using what exists, at every stage we are exploiting the *really creative* power of the vital, we are embroidering on the pre-existent frame which is the real masterpiece, we are ingeniously making use of the genius of the cells and, in so doing, we are rather like revue artists who win cheap applause by parodying a scene from *Le Cid* or a speech from *Cyrano de Bergerac* . . . Let us take care not to claim all the glory of the success we have obtained. In our most striking, most spectacular experiments the chief part of the spectacle is supplied by life – life the anonymous. 'We have gone a long way for men,' as Montesquieu said. Let us not forget that phrase 'for men'. And let us not give ourselves the airs of demigods, or even of demiurges, when we have merely been petty magicians.

★

Shall we, one of these days, understand these powers of life, these creative and organising powers upon which we try our hand with more or less luck? Should a complete comprehension of the phenomenon of the vital be counted among the reasonable hopes of biology?

Man has so often crossed frontiers that seemed impossible and science has so often made a mock of the 'No Trespassers' board, that one would be tempted to give the answer 'yes' and to bet on it. But from the fact that mankind has raised up so many false barriers would it be right to conclude that it will never come up against real ones? Certainly we must not rule out any dream, even the boldest; but if, after all, life is – as some people think – a primal datum that cannot be reduced to the complexities of physico-chemistry, and if the great gap is situated, as Bergson suggested, between the inert and the vital, then we shall not remake life, and it will for ever remain to us a mystery . . .

And I believe that that is precisely where the marvellous, fascinating, tragic interest of biology resides: in the uncertainty of its very subject matter, in the ambiguity of its elements, in the indefiniteness of its hopes. If we were perfectly sure, from now on, that life is merely an effect of matter, if we were perfectly sure that, even in a distant future, we were bound to succeed in synthesising it in our test tubes, if there did not, on this subject, persist that shadow of doubt which cannot help insinuating itself even into the most established certainty, then I think we would be less greedy to raise the veil: I think we would not be so tremulously eager, so deeply moved, every time a fresh success comes along to confirm our hopefulness, every time we receive from a mystery something that looks like a sign of encouragement . . . 'You would seek me with less fervour,' life might say to the biologist, 'if you were sure of finding me.'

One might even, I believe, go so far as to say, without being paradoxical, that every biologist, however faithful to mechanistic theories, is an unconscious vitalist. Why, after all, should he have chosen this strange profession, which consists in scrutinising the evidences of vitality, if he did not attribute, at least deep down in his sub-conscious mind, a privileged value to the living thing? It is in proportion as he attaches value to the vital that he strives obstinately to reduce it, and his ambition to possess it is the measure of his respect for it.

*

Whatever may be the last word on the enigma of life, the destiny of the biologist is bound to be an impressive one. Either he will in the end manufacture life, recreate organic structure – in which case, as the author of a new nature, he will place himself on an equality with the gods. Or his efforts will be disappointed indefinitely, he will always come up against the unknown – in which case he will at least have had the signal glory of manipulating what cannot be created, of playing with the divine.

For my part, if I had to pronounce on what life is, I would simply say that my surprise at its works and at its patterns has never ceased to grow and is still – I can feel it – in its phase of increase.

A science, however fast moving, develops less quickly than the impatience of an individual mind. The amount of progress, the number of discoveries and victories there have been since the time – it seems far off yet is very close – of my adolescence! The whole of experimental biology, practically speaking, has been built up under my eyes. And I have to confess, none the less, that an exhaustive understanding of the vital seems to me today much more arduous than it appeared to my juvenile fervour.

The longer, the more assiduously one has lived on familiar terms with living things, the more one feels out-distanced, bewildered and put to shame . . . Yes, put to shame by the generosity of life with its teeming resources; by its way of moving ahead, nearly always, in a different manner from that which our petty human logic would have foreseen; by the way in which life ceaselessly shows up the inadequacy of our rational vocabulary and refuses to let itself be shut up within our descriptive or regulatory concepts; by the way in which life – as the philosopher Cournot put it so profoundly – is at one and the same time 'so much more and so much less than man'; by the way in which life, which we pretend to imitate with our 'feedbacks' and all their elaborate ironmongery, puts more industry and art into the least of its protoplasms than there is in our computers that take a whole building to house them; by the power life has of packing into a blob of transparent albumen what man would be incapable of cramming into a factory, and of lodging in the minute brain of the bee the memory of a dance that is a language; by the fact that life must *also* be given all the credit for what is achieved by her daughter, thought;

by this life which disconcerts us just as much in the quivering antherozooid of a fern as in the torments of the human heart, and has contrived to pass gently, without a break, from tropism to genius, from the microbe to Pasteur, from a mould to Fleming and from the plant to Goethe; by the way in which life accomplishes every day, beneath our eyes, the overwhelming miracle of producing a man out of an invisible germ cell; and finally by the fact that life would *merely be more prodigious still* if it should prove to have done all this with the first thing that lay to hand, and to have put on for us so fine a show of the incomprehensible with no other resources than the knowable . . .

★

Every science has its particular message, and it is natural that the specialist should rather complacently stress the one that emanates from his own discipline. Astronomy, Henri Poincaré used to say, tells us of Man's material smallness and spiritual grandeur; by revealing to us the existence of simple and fixed laws at the base of a universal harmony it has made our souls capable of comprehending the world. As for geology, according to Termier it shows us our planet in continual movement and teaches us, by this, the instability and fleetingness of things.

Of biology one may say, provisionally, that it is distinguished by the extremely specific quality of its subject matter. Speaking of living organisms, the great Claude Bernard said: 'We must not read into them either a chemical retort or a soul: *we must read into them what is there.*' And that excellent epigram contains a criticism both of indolent vitalist theories and of crude mechanistic ones.

Being heavily charged with the irrational (in Meyerson's sense of the word), biology is assuredly the least mathematical of the sciences, and without question the least amenable to mathematics, because it is the richest in concrete content. It is the one that lends itself least to the enterprises of pure logic. Its whole history is there to remind us how gross were the mistakes made by the theorists, beginning with Descartes, who claimed to draw an explanation of vital phenomena from a few principles set up *a priori*. Life is essentially that which does not let its secret be pierced and can only be studied decently by dint of keeping in perpetual contact with the swarming of facts.

Since it is not, or is to so small an extent, a deductive science, biology is considered by some people as a young, immature, *minor* science, that has not yet acquired the appearance of true science. They hold that it is, for that reason, a mediocre 'introduction to knowledge'.[1] I think, on the contrary, that it is, for

[1] 'The biologist does what he can, but it is not much ... It is advisable to be sceptical about his ideas of reality, since he is always up against the concrete. Biology is in consequence a decidedly mediocre "introduction to the knowledge of the human mind", almost as mediocre as that of Vauvenargues (1746), and the philosophers who quote Claude Bernard on every occasion have a very rudimentary idea of scientific method and the scientific spirit.' (Marcel Boll, Optimisme et Pessimisme, *La Raison militante.*)

this very reason, an irreplaceable element in human-istic education. I think it is bound to supply a counter-poise to the teachings of the other sciences, which would end by persuading us that the universe is nothing but an immense blackboard covered with rows of figures and formulae. I think that the study of the mysterious 'what is there' of Claude Bernard's phrase is well adapted to expand and enrich the intelligence. A spurting, juicy, fleshy, tangible, even sensuous science, biology is complementary to the desiccations and emaciations of mathematics.

Shall I go further and say that in so far as biology is recalcitrant to mathematics, it yields us something other than the reflected image of our own mind? It gives us the opportunity of admiring the real without glassing ourselves in it. It is the least self-centred, the least nar-cissistic of the sciences – the one that, by taking us out of ourselves, leads us to re-establish a link with nature and to shake ourselves free from our spiritual isolation.

★

And yet, this same biology, which sets man in rela-tion with the inhuman, is certainly, by its implications, applications and consequences, the most human science there is.

Is it not already beginning to introduce itself into our daily life, into our bread winning, our customs and our laws? Did I not read in the papers, not long ago, that expert analysis of the blood had now acquired legal importance as a means of deciding paternity?

Was it not by biological tests that it proved possible, the other day, to rediscover the identity of two children who, when new born, had been substituted for one another in a maternity home?

The best way to gain an idea of what the human, *emotional* value of biology can be, is to look through the strange correspondence that a biologist receives . . . People take him for a magician, a healer, a confessor, a friend . . . And this is at one and the same time, comic and touching, as almost everything is that comes from deep down in human beings. Here we have a couple who have lost their little girl whom they adored, and would like to have another child, but on condition that it is again a girl and is like the first one in every feature . . . Here we have a man who is in love with a half-caste girl and is thinking of marrying her but on condition that it can be guaranteed that she will not give him children who are darker than she is . . . This letter is about a man and woman, first cousins, who want to marry but are afraid of the effects of inbreeding on their descendants . . . This is from a young woman with scruples, who is afraid of transmitting a congenital cataract . . . Here is one from a jealous husband who, having blue eyes like his wife, is amazed at having a child with dark eyes and begs to be reassured that the laws of Mendel are fallible . . . Here we have a man who would like to prove, by a blood count, that he is not the father of the child that is imputed to him . . . And another who would like, by the same means, to get hold of a child that is being denied him . . . A simpleton who would love to be able to think there are pregnancies that last longer than ten months . . . And the parents who would like at any price to give their children a little more intelligence . . . And the children who would like at any price to prolong the life of an ageing parent . . . And the old people obsessed by the dream of rejuvenation . . . And all the people discontented with themselves, who would like to grow an inch or two taller or make their hair grow again . . . And the ones who would find it convenient to change sex, in order to get their bodily formation into harmony with their deranged instincts . . . And the mature women who, desiring to make use of the few ova that remain to them, beg for the means of a last-moment fruitfulness . . . And the lonely old maids who, having now no hope except from artificial insemination, would like to be supplied with a guaranteed brand of human seed . . . No, indeed, the science that provokes such appeals, prayers and confessions, the science that penetrates into private life, and whose warnings or advice can influence a marriage, a decision to have children, a person's destiny, is no ordinary science.

For the moment, biology is incapable of satisfying the principal requests addressed to it by the man in the street. It does not prolong life, it does not determine sex, it does not control heredity, it does not procure intelligence for fools . . . But it is possible that all these powers may belong to it tomorrow, and many others as well, which people do not dream of expecting from it: the procreation of twins at will, test tube pregnancy, the modification of the embryo, controlled mutations, the production of a superhuman being . . .

c

Under the magic wand of biology, man is now gradually becoming quite different from what he was. Here and now he is changing into a new and paradoxical animal, unknown to those who assign names to things, an animal with a special, pied physiology, borrowing features from the most diverse families of the animal kingdom. Here and now *Homo sapiens* is in process of becoming *Homo biologicus* – a strange biped that will combine the properties of self-reproduction without males, like the green-fly, of fertilising his female at long distance like the nautiloid molluscs, of changing sex like the xiphophores, of growing from cuttings like the earth-worm, of replacing its missing parts like the newt, of developing outside the mother's body like the kangaroo, and of hibernating like the hedgehog.

*

In his *Brave New World* Aldous Huxley has shown us a society dominated by biological technocracy. I have very often been asked if I considered that we were on the way towards such a world.

On the way? But surely we are there already, without knowing it . . . Is not a human race which has seen three babies emerge from vitrified semen, in which the severing of nerve fibres in the lobes of the brain in order to modify the personality is a daily occurrence, and in which hormones are daily used to promote growth and to balance temperament or sexuality, already a 'biologised' humanity?

Such an expansion of the power of man over man is

bound, indeed, to cause us some uneasiness. So far we have been concerned merely to show the victories and hopes of biology. We shall come later to the disquieting problems which it raises.

II

MAN AND SCIENCE

ALTHOUGH TO APPLY A DESCRIPTIVE epithet to the period in which one lives is to risk ridicule, I scarcely think I shall arouse any protest by the statement that we are living now in a Scientific Age. To say so is by no means to attribute crudely some sort of spiritual or moral primacy to science, but merely, without the slightest attempt at a value judgment and without any prejudice in favour of science, to point out a state of fact. Whether we like it or not, whether we glory in it or deplore it, science holds a considerable place in our societies, and one that is ceaselessly expanding. As M. Pierre Frieden has well said, in a remarkable speech which he made at Luxembourg recently, science has today become 'the first great power in the world'.

Obviously it would never enter anybody's head to say that we are passing through an age of poetry . . . Nor even an age of philosophy, in spite of the success of existentialism. And I do not believe, in spite of the vogue for Marxism, that it would be any truer to find the essential characteristic of our period in the embitterment of ideologies; for these may prove to be only a passing manifestation, whereas we cannot, from now on, at least in our own cycle of civilisation, conceive of a period in which science would lose its power and its prestige.

From what moment in human history must we date this scientific age, which is our own?

Charles Galton-Darwin, the grandson of the illustrious author of the *Origin of Species*, distinguishes four fundamental phases in the evolution of humanity: the age of fire, the age of agriculture, the age of towns, and finally the age of science. This last age has been preparing since Greek antiquity – perhaps indeed it was preparing long before that, since its origin is indistinguishable from the awakening of intellectual curiosity; but one may agree, rather roughly, that its real start was in the seventeenth century, which saw the birth of the methods that are capable of leading to scientific invention and discovery. At that moment the human mind adopted towards the universe an entirely different attitude from the one which had been in force up till then. Submitting to the school of facts, it observed natural phenomena patiently, instead of trying to guess them at one go by means of its reason. This docility, this modesty, this renunciation, this resignation to temporary ignorance, were destined to result in an immediate increase of knowledge and of power. From that time onwards discoveries and inventions, which till then had cropped up irregularly and sporadically, were to multiply and abound. First there came impressive but purely theoretical revelations, such as the discovery of the law of gravity and the construction of a system of the universe. But soon there arose novelties of more interest to the man in the street, discoveries which, by modifying the conditions of everyday life, were to make everybody realise that science is not merely a toy for the curious, or an instrument of meditation for specialists, but a material force which has to be reckoned with and may be expected to yield power, riches, security and even pleasure.

One of the first manifestations of science to make a vivid impression on public opinion was the discovery of anaesthesia, round about 1850. To abolish pain – even at the dentist's – was no small thing. Then came, with Pasteur, the discovery of microbes which upset the whole of medicine; that of vaccination against infectious diseases; Lister's discovery of antisepsis, and then Terrier's of aseptic treatment, following which surgery was able to begin its beneficent ascent. Let us not forget that, less than a century ago, surgery was scarcely ever more than a sinister trade, so much so that the recruitment of young surgeons was becoming practically impossible. Jean-Louis Faure has told the nightmare story of that small villa at Meudon to which, in 1860 or thereabouts, the celebrated Nélaton brought fifteen young women, to try out upon them the removal of a fibrous tumour: all fifteen of them died, legally assassinated by the learned and innocent Landru. The villa was nicknamed by the neighbours the House of Crime!

Then came, in 1894, the first injections of anti-diphtheria serum. Thanks to the joint efforts of Behring and Dr. Roux, croup was conquered, and the lives of thousands of children were saved. At that moment there was, at least in France, a prodigious surge of enthusiasm: it was, indeed, one of the first occasions on which, awakened by the press, the masses were excited by a scientific fact and began to realise clearly what the laboratory can offer to mankind. Almost at the same time, in Germany, the Würtzburg doctor, Röntgen, was busy discovering the miraculous rays that pass through the flesh and make it possible for anyone to watch his own skeleton moving. Then came the discovery, by the Curies, of radium, the 'fabulous metal' which seemed to upset all the laws of the conservation of energy. And meanwhile thousands of industrial applications of science were becoming visible: chemical synthesis, electric light, transformation of the means of communication and transport, etc.

But to provide a picture of the evolution of science and all its technical consequences is no part of our present purpose; let us simply note here that, by 1900, the prodigy of science was installed in the midst of our society as master. Now, in the 1950s, there is no longer any victory of science that could astonish us. We expect everything of it – and perhaps, above all, the unexpected.

If it is true, as Voltaire said, that magic is the art of doing what nature cannot do, science has taken rank as positive magic. Every day – on the planes of power, speed and health – a fresh miracle is offered to us.

Every day some fresh enterprise against space, time or death. Now it is the cure for an incurable disease, or surgery daring to attack an organ which one would have thought untouchable. Now it is artificial hibernation, the splitting of the atom, television, cybernetics, the crossing of the wall of sound, the bathyscaph, the photographing of the electron, the analysis of stellar radiations, the curing of madness by electric shocks, the modification of personality by brain surgery, the transformation of sex or the production of animals without a father.

Hardly have we digested one of these marvels when a new one is set before us! And not only the practical world, the world of action, but also the world of representation and thought, finds itself modified. In what universe will one wake up tomorrow? From one morning to the next, we learn that space is closed instead of being infinite, that the spiral nebulae are twice as far away as they were thought to be, that the human species is ten times older, that causality has proved bankrupt, or that it is once again triumphant . . .

Surprise has become so familiar to us that we are beginning to be blasé. The cure of tuberculosis by means of streptomycin has had a distinctly less warm welcome than that of diphtheria fifty years before. Already we accept the benefits lavished by science with the slightly weary nonchalance of a spoilt child who is given beautiful toys. Or rather, people are inclined to complain when, on some particular point, science is too slow in playing its part as magician! Its munificence has, so to speak, spoilt the market. What! have

they not yet solved the problem of cancer? Have they
not yet conquered the common cold? But what are
they up to, then, in the laboratories?

Yes, of science everything is expected: people believe
that, to it, all things are possible. It must make dwarfs
grow tall, it must dispense eternal youth, it must supply
wit to imbeciles, it must raise the dead.

To give an example: a few months ago, a young
journalist came to see me, to interview me on some
subject or other; and, to start the conversation, he
asked me: 'You are the man who has manufactured a
calf, aren't you?' – in the same tone of voice in which
he would have asked whether it was I who had pub-
lished a certain book, or exhibited a certain picture.

To these men of little science, the men of science,
there is a tendency to attribute omniscience. Because I
myself have experimented on the generation of frogs
and have written a certain number of books on biology
people do not hesitate to consult me about the most
diverse questions, which range from the destruction of
beauty spots to the longevity of parents or the existence
of God.

In our scientific age, science penetrates into all fields:
the military art, police, the choice of professions,
nutritional technique, expert study of works of art, the
detection of frauds, etc. It intervenes in matters of house-
keeping or matters of personal feeling. Biology is used
in order to identify a criminal or to decide a law suit
about paternity. Whether a child is or is not heir to a
fortune may depend on the result of a blood analysis.

Helping now towards sterility, now towards fertility, and providing information on the state of pregnancy before any swelling can be seen, science has its word to say on the fate of families. The fertilising needle enters into morals, it is provided for and paid for under social insurance, and already one receives pieces of paste-board with such inscriptions as: 'Mlle X has the pleasure of announcing the birth of her daughter [or son] by artificial insemination.' The church, in the person of Father Riquet, is striving to reconcile biology and the Gospels, and the Vatican thinks itself obliged to use the language of genetics and microbiology in its encyclicals. Princesses productive of daughters consult specialists in sexual mutation in the hope of getting from them the secret of how to bear sons; and, in the case of some dynasty subject to haemophilia, efforts are made to track down the fatal chromosome that hinders the coagulation of royal blood.

Medical science, by prolonging old age, is modifying expectation of life – so much so that the payers of life annuities and the candidates for election to academies are growing alarmed, and the government, when it thinks of postponing the pensionable age, is forced to give penicillin as its excuse.

Science is invading literature through 'science fiction' – for which, to speak for myself, I have little taste, since I prefer the mysterious glow of truth to all the ex-cessively logical consequences that are deduced from it. However, it seems there is no lack of readers for these fantastic stories in which Supermen travelling faster than light lose years as they change galaxies!

Science now goes on the stage. In André Roussin's farce *Lorsque l'enfant paraît* one of the torrentially plentiful pregnancies which form the subject of the play is revealed by the 'rabbit's reaction'. (Roussin is, indeed, not quite up to date, for nowadays it is the frog, rather than the rabbit, that is used to test pregnancy.) And have we not seen a member of the Académie Goncourt, M. Philippe Hériat, in his *Immaculée*, treat brilliantly the grave subject of human parthenogenesis?

Science lends its aid to publicity, and this is perhaps one of the best proofs of the prestige it has with the masses. To secure its adoption by feminine vanity a beauty cream must contain (or claim to contain!) sexual hormones or extract of chicken embryo, or again – the latest fashion, this – 'royal jelly'! On the beauty-treatment market there now appear electronic waxes, radioactive mudpacks, blended hormone pastes, lotions with a special yeast basis; lipsticks have to be colloidal, cleansing creams to be synthesised, brilliantines to be aerosol, shampoos to be vitaminised, facepowders to be dynamised or micronised!

Even the craze for false sciences is a symptom of this scientific age of ours. For none of those charlatans and super-humbugs – the soothsayers, fakirs, astrologers, magi, spiritualists, radiant healers, metapsychists and occultists – forgets to dress up his ancient mania in the fashionable garb of the new science. The talk among these sorcerers is of nothing but radiations, wave lengths, induction fields, vibrations, interference and remanence! It is faith-healer's digest, a hotch potch of electro-magneticism and wave mechanics compiled for the use of simpletons. And confronted by the success of these impostors, confronted by the prosperity of all these exploiters of human distress and credulity, one is driven to wonder whether the age of science is not also, inevitably, the age of false science. When everything is possible, why not everything that anybody says? When there are wireless waves, why not waves sent out by the human brain? When there is television, why not clairvoyance? When there are cosmic rays, why not astral influences? When there is the splitting of matter, why not the ectoplasms of the mediums?

Only a fairly advanced scientific education can enable people to discriminate between the true marvels and the false. In some respects, one may well say, the vulgarisation of science, which is none the less so necessary, is bound to present a certain danger. Reality and lies are found side by side in the weeklies with large circulations: readers find in them, on the same page, under headlines of the same type, the account of a magnificent discovery and a stupid story about a haunted house!

And let us not forget, at the same time, that – because of the specialisation, which is becoming more and more obligatory – nobody can master all the knowledge of our time. This admirable science of ours does not exist in any single human brain: on the contrary, on most of the subjects that are foreign to his own field, the man of science himself is reduced to judging in ignorance. And finally, we find that the idolatry of science – unhealthy like all idolatry – plays into the hands of imposture. As the philosopher Jaspers says: 'The man who believes in the all-powerfulness of science yields first place to the specialists, but at the first set-back he turns away from them, disillusioned, and addresses himself to the charlatans.' This is one of the reasons for the success of the healers – who do indeed make genuine cures of certain bodily disorders of nervous origin, but by means that have nothing mysterious about them and are known to the science of psychoanalysis.

★

However that may be, and notwithstanding the success of the false sciences which may be regarded as one more homage paid by the false to the true, I think it is permissible to say that, on the whole, the prestige of genuine science is still growing. There is at present no other form of activity which inspires in public opinion so much confidence and awakens so much hope . . .

And, effective and important as this science already is, it is only at the very beginning of its development. The scientific age has only just begun: it has been going on for scarcely three centuries, and we have before us thousands of millions of years, if not millions of millions, in which to find out and make new things. In an enquiry carried out not long ago by *Les Nouvelles littéraires*, which took as its starting-point a paragraph by Jules Romains, all the scientists who were questioned agreed in rejecting the idea that the principal truths were behind us and that the number of discoveries of the first magnitude was bound to become smaller and smaller.

To mention only some of the long-standing hopes of mankind, it can hardly be doubted that science will achieve interplanetary navigation, and will put off the maturing of old age and of death . . . What is more, by modifying reality, it will arouse the mind to further hopes, to hopes of which today the idea could not enter our heads; for the work of science – as Victor Hugo said of God – always 'goes far beyond our dream'.

And yet there is a question that arises: will humanity last long enough to let science advance to the limit of its possibilities? Shall we not soon be short of fuel? Oil is nearly exhausted, and it seems that tomorrow it will be the turn of coal . . . And will not food run short, in a century or two or a millennium or two, when the population in every part of the world keeps on growing as a result of the progress of medicine?

I do not think it is unduly optimistic to state categorically that science is capable of dealing with these threats. It will be able to draw upon fresh sources of energy, and to invent a fresh means of subsistence. The same ingenuity, the same subtlety that has found out how to increase the quantity of human protoplasm on the world's surface will shortly find the secret of how to keep this additional humanity alive – or, if necessary, to limit the numbers of the earth's inhabitants, and this without shameful recourse to regulation by massacre.

Yes, science will be able to create for itself the time necessary for the amplification and development of its work. But it does seem to be coming up against a natural limit, inherent in the very structure of the human brain. Is not man, by virtue of the nature of his

D

cerebral apparatus, condemned not to go beyond a certain level of understanding? If the eye, and indeed all the sense organs, are imperfect sources of information, why should the central reservoir of sensory information be gifted with complete perfection?

We know, of course, that primitive men – Mauer Man, or even Neanderthal Man – those animal men with their low receding foreheads and huge jaws, would not have been able to solve, still less to raise, a thousandth part of the problems raised and solved by their successor, *Homo sapiens*. And as for our ancestor, Pithecanthropus, he may not even have got as far as the age of fire. What follows? Can so slight a modification of the brain – the enlargement of certain lobes, the increase of the weight of the hemispheres by a pound, the addition of a few degrees of width of the facial angle – have made intelligence pass from nearly zero to infinity? It does not seem very probable.

Yet if, apparently, the conformation of the human brain sets a limit to the progress of science, we are now forced to realise that this limit itself may be widened by the fact that man has, for some time now, not been the only creature on earth to accomplish his task – the task of a thinking being. He has, in fact, found himself powerful auxiliaries. These auxiliaries are the 'thinking machines' – those extraordinary mechanisms whose genesis will be seen to mark a fresh stage in human development, a sub-age of the scientific age: the age of 'artificial thought', as Pierre de Latil has put it.

The ancestor of these thinking machines – and compared to them it is as man's small reptilian ancestor to man – was the counting machine which Blaise Pascal as a young man invented in about 1642 to make it easier to do his father's accounts. It was capable of doing 'all sorts of operations without pen and paper or counters, without knowing any of the rules of arithmetic, and with infallible accuracy'. This prehistoric machine of Pascal's, which made a sensation at the time and was even hailed by the poets, was extremely rudimentary by the side of the enormous machines we possess today. These do far better than the working out of simple sums, for they can carry out all kinds of derivation and integration and solve every sort of algebraic equation, even the most complex ones, swarming with unknown factors. It is just as if these machines were gifted with the powers of reflection and memory, and were capable of real logical reasoning. Guillaume Apollinaire wrote in *Calligrammes*:

> *Ordre du temps si les machines*
> *Se prenaient enfin à penser.*

Well, it has happened: machines, from now on, do think, and it is essential to realise the gigantic implications of this event – to which, as to all the applications of science, people are already beginning to get accustomed before they have fully savoured its fantastic meaning.

We were, of course, already quite used to seeing man surpassed and beaten by machines on the strictly material plane, on the plane of dexterity, strength and rapidity . . . We were familiar with elegant mechanisms which carried out automatically acts of choice, or tests, or combinations of movements finally adjusted to a given end, and all this far more precisely and regularly than any human being could have done. We used currently the expression 'as good as machine-made'; but everyone must see that the extraordinary machines mentioned above are quite another matter. By them, man finds himself equalled and even beaten and out-classed, in a field that seemed to be specifically and by choice his own, a field that we had every right to believe was reserved to him for ever. We must now get used to saying 'as good as machine-thought', meaning that we have an extra guarantee of accuracy.

Let us quickly look at a few details of these artificial brains. One of them – the well known E.N.I.A.C. (the initials stand for Electronic Numeral Interpoler Automatic Computer) was made in America in 1946 or thereabouts. It took two years to build, with the collaboration of two hundred scientists, and it cost $750,000; it weighs thirty tons and has 500,000 parts, including 18,000 electronic tubes. This inert and shining thinker can solve in a fraction of a second an equation with a hundred unknown factors. It can polish off in a few minutes a piece of work in mathematical logic that would have taken an expert human calculator ten years, working eight hours a day. In less than an hour it completes work that would occupy a whole human life. And these prodigies, these exploits, are obtained without the slightest fatigue or wear and with a ridiculously small expenditure of energy.

E.N.I.A.C. has now numerous rivals in various parts of the world. Their total calculating power far exceeds that of all human beings put together. And the importance of these machines is being confirmed and extended continuously; they already intervene in the most varied fields of speculation and of practical application – pure mathematics, astronomy, chemistry, meteorology, technology and industry. They help to decide the characteristics of an aeroplane, to work out critical speeds or complex trajectories, to anticipate the times of tides, to calculate accurately the distribution of atmospheric pressures, to show the structure of a molecule, to assign its place to an atom in a crystal, to explore the field of prime numbers, to try out fresh logical combinations, to deduce the remote consequences of a hypothesis, to reckon the costs of an enterprise, to establish a budget.

On the other hand there are – luckily for human self-respect! – a fair number of problems which neither E.N.I.A.C. nor any of its electronic colleagues is capable of solving. And it is easy to understand that this confrontation – this competition, if I may put it that way – between the flesh and blood brain and the metal brain is a fascinating and extremely disquieting subject. It must lead us to make, within what we have till now lumped together as 'thought', a distinction between the purely logical – in which a machine excels and triumphs – and the inventive, the creative, the only part from which, it seems the machine is excluded and in which the intervention of man is essential.

Wiener, who is one of the masters of the science of cybernetics, or science of self-governed mechanisms, has set himself to draw up the inventory, the catalogue, of those mental acts which the human brain seems to be alone capable of accomplishing, and of which it seems likely to keep – until some fresh development – the monopoly.

And so, if we want to define and isolate that which is 'proper to man', to compare him with the animal from which he derives is now no longer our only resource. We can – and we must – also compare him with the machines which he builds. 'Human' will mean not merely that of which no beast is capable, but that which exceeds the power of any machine.

And so the devotees of cybernetics allow to man no more than a quite small range within which he cannot be replaced by machinery: even now they have in mind super E.N.I.A.C.s that would have the power to solve all problems, so that the only superiority of the flesh and blood brain would be that of setting the problems – and also, let us not forget, that of making the machines with the power to solve them.

To digress for a moment: some experts in cybernetics, struck by the likenesses in the behaviour of machine and man, draw the conclusion that there is a deeply-lying similarity of structure and organisation. Improving on La Mettrie's *homme-machine* and on the marionnette man of Le Dantec, they go so far as to maintain that the human brain is, after all, only a thinking-machine that is conscious of existing. And they bring forward to support this thesis those strange artificial animals which, by means of the complexity of their self-regulating mechanisms, strikingly imitate the spontaneity and caprices of living creatures: for instance, Elmer and Elsie, Grey Walter's two electronic tortoises, which crawl, move forwards, stop, move backwards, respond to light, appear to follow and to search, attract or repel one another, and, when they are tired – that is to·say, when their batteries run down, go of their own accord and plug in to the source of energy which will give them movement again.

Other artificial beasts complete the disquieting fauna: the Coras – again made by Grey Walter – Pierre Ducrocq's fox, etc. Some of them are able to learn, to acquire conditioned reflexes, that is to say, to associate two stimuli in a new way, so much so that their behaviour turns out to be unforeseeable even by the human demiurge who brought them into the world and knows their secret workings. What, by the side of these electronic bags of tricks, are the automata of the past – Archytas's pigeon, or Vaucanson's duck, although it could waddle and swim, quack, spread its wings, swallow pieces of bread, digest them and evacuate them in the normal way? One is reminded rather of the automata of legend or of dreams, such as the artificial man that is supposed to have been made by Albertus Magnus and smashed by St Thomas because he took it for a creature of the devil; or the Future Eve that sprang from the brain of Villiers de l'Isle-Adam.

Those who have read his marvellous story will remember the seductive 'Androïde' which the magician Edison substituted for a woman of flesh and blood in order to save a highly romantic young English lord from suicide. Villiers' Future Eve was not yet electronic, but she contained golden phonographs stocked – although long playing records were not yet invented – with hours of fine speech (are not a hundred phrases enough to meet any situation of the heart?), and wax cylinders inscribed with seventy movements, expressions and attitudes (which is far in excess of the variety necessary to a well brought up woman, for twenty-seven or twenty-eight are already the sign of an exceptional personality). The Count of Villiers raised, with the cruel irony of a great poet, the whole problem of the relations between the natural and the artificial, between the living and the mechanical. This problem has now become singularly acute, since intelligent people are wondering very seriously whether the robots of cybernetics do not present us with a valid image of life and of thought.

For my part, I reject such an analogy. I do not believe that these magnificent but coarse imitations give us any better information on the vital and the spiritual than did the osmotic plants of Stéphane Leduc about vegetable growth. The manufacture of the smallest grain of assimilant albumen would mean much more to me than all this portentous ironmongery; and, much as I marvel at the reasoning mastodons, I admire much more the tiny human brain, which is born from a single cell and can be seen any day forming itself from a puckering of the ectoderm.

But, whatever one may think of the explanatory value of the logic machines taken as *models of the thinking organ*, it is none the less true that they are capable of being valuable collaborators with the human brain, sparing it energy and time. Changing the famous phrase from Villiers de l'Isle-Adam's *Axel*, the man of the future will be able to say: 'Think! Our servants can do that for us.'

We are going to be more and more dependent on these soulless oracles. We shall rely on them more and more for every effort of abstraction and reasoning, for all purely reflective and logical work, for all the mechanical drudgery of intelligence. And thus freed from the load of the accessory and the burden of the secondary, the human spirit will have all its forces available for the tasks that are worthy of it and will be able to devote itself to what is essential – in a way, to specialise in genius.

★

Besides, there is another way in which science can help to make sure of its own continual development. Biology can, in fact, set to work to modify the organ of thought itself – the living brain, the flesh and blood brain. And it is this that has made it possible to say that 'the science that can, if need be, modify the organ responsible for all science is no ordinary science'.

To bring into the world a man superior to the men of today – a 'superman' – has been the dream of philosophers, from Nietzsche's *Zarathustra*, to Renan's *Dialogues philosophiques*.[1] To make it come true, a methodical selection of those individuals best gifted with intellectual faculties might be considered: it is probable that in this

[1] See Chapter III.

way we would get, in a few generations, men of more than average intelligence, and possible that among them would be found men superior to anything we have yet known. As long as no such selection has been tried, nobody has the right to assign limits to human genius. All we know, after all, is natural man, seedling man, and it might well turn out that the best men of this sort are, compared to the models still dormant within the species, no more than the wild pears of the woodlands, with their small, sour, uneatable fruit, to the huge William pears that melt in one's mouth.

Of course, human selection would be directed at improving, not the logical faculties of the mind, which have lost a great deal of their value now that we know they can be replaced by machinery, but the properly human faculties of creation and invention.

This is not the place for a discussion of the practical difficulties – the social and moral ones – which the employment of selective measures would come up against. Perhaps man will never make up his mind, even for the sake of raising himself higher through the spirit, to practise methods that appear to him too much contrary to his dignity: perhaps he will reject the superman out of scruple . . . But germinal selection is only one of the means of improvement open to him. The artificial stimulation of favourable mutations may also be considered: so may – and this is, I think, less Utopian – a variety of physiological treatments which would be confined to modifying individuals without touching the heredity of the species. In this way we would produce supermen without creating Superman. The treatment would have to be renewed for each generation, since there is – at least within the time-limits accessible to experiment – no hereditary transmission of modification acquired by the individual.

On these lines, we could try modifying the brain of the young child, which is still plastic and unfinished, or, better still, that of the embryo, with a view to causing an increase in the number of brain cells, or of favouring the irrigation of the brain with blood,[1] or of accentuating that lack of symmetry between the hemispheres of the brain which appears to be somewhat generally associated with intellectual superiority.[2]

More simply, one might also bring to bear on the adult brain chemical substances – hormones or catalysts – that would stimulate its working. Maxiton, the orthedrins, the vitamins and glutamic acid are already known and it can hardly be doubted that better things of the kind will be discovered. There is no *a priori* reason why we should not succeed in stimulating the working of the brain just as we at present do with other less exalted vital parts.[3]

[1] According to Dr Huidzie, brain power seems to depend on the calibre and complexity of the blood vessels nourishing the brain.   [2] See the next chapter.

[3] According to Krech, Rosenzweig, Bennett and Madame Kruckel, there appears to be more cholinesterase in the brains of the cleverer specimens of the rat – that is to say, in those that find their way mainly by a sense of direction (the ones more disposed to react to visual impressions being considered less intelligent). Cholinesterase is an enzyme which acts on acetylcholine, a chemical substance that plays an important part in the functioning of nervous tissue. (See *Science*, 1954, 120, p. 994; also 'Le Rôle de

Even if the use of these future drugs resulted in no more than a few minutes of 'superthought' per day, and if these flashes were paid for by long periods of depression, mankind would still find it worthwhile to procure them, since we know now that thought can be seconded by machines over the greater part of its work and that the irreplaceable human contribution is, in quantity, quite small.

Whatever the methods used to increase the output of the flesh and blood brain, we are entitled to hope that, out of the collaboration between living creativeness and the infallible logic of the machine, a 'superscience' will be born, even more penetrating, subtle and efficient than the science of today. If this superscience in turn invents its own methods of bringing the thinking machines – the natural ones as well as the artificial – still closer to perfection, it is plain that, from progress to progress, from one advance to another, science may go on expanding indefinitely.

Man has here a reason for enthusiasm and pride. On the scientific plane we have now the right to a complete optimism: the future will be sown thick with marvels, it will overflow with prodigies. It certainly looks as if the evolution of science were relaying the advance of life itself, which seems to have reached the end of its lap. It certainly looks as if the vast ascending movement of animal life were being prolonged in the human brain with the aid of its lifeless collaborators.

l'élément cholinergique', by B. Minz, *Biologie médicale*, August-September, 1955.)

Fr. Teilhard de Chardin, scientist and Christian, sees in this apotheosis of science something that, by approaching the divine, brings to the spirit an honour and a satisfaction far beyond the pleasures of power and security: 'To know more, to be able to do more – these words, though for many they still have a utilitarian meaning, are haloed, for everybody, with a sacred value.'

★

It would be surprising if no sober consideration came along to modify so general an optimism. It would be abnormal if so bright a medal had no reverse side . . .

Is this triumphal ascent of science free from disadvantages? Does it not create certain dangers?

Let us, to begin with, set aside certain superficial criticisms. Science, it is sometimes said, cures some diseases but gives rise to others: if bacterial infections have in our time been more or less conquered, infections by virus are increasing in frequency, and so are heart diseases, cancer and neuroses – not to mention the numerous deaths that are the result of technical progress, itself a consequence of the progress of science.

The answer to objections of this sort can be read clearly in the statistics of mortality. In every country the population is steadily increasing, in spite of murderous wars: so much so, indeed, that it is becoming a subject of uneasiness. Therefore, if the expansion of life is the criterion, the balance of science is clearly a favourable one; and Jean-Jacques Rousseau could no longer, in an attempt to defend barbarism, apostrophise the scientist as he did in 1750 in his famous *Discours sur les sciences et les arts*: 'If you, from whom we have received so many sublime forms of knowledge, had taught us none of these things, would there be any fewer of us alive?'

Criticism of science as the cause of a machine civilisation is more specious; but here we really must distinguish between the results of machinery itself and the results of its misuse. That mechanisation is at present an instrument of the enslavement of some classes of society is a fact beyond doubt, but it is no less certain that the fault lies with the defects of our social organisation. If in our day the machine overwhelms and crushes man instead of liberating him, this is because – to use an excellent phrase of Paul Langevin's – justice has lagged behind science; and, instead of accusing the too rapid advance of science, we might do better to deplore the slow advance of justice.

Then comes another objection, a contradictory one: what will happen to men when, having been replaced by machines, they have been relieved of the time-honoured obligation to work? What will they do with their interminable leisure, their unlimited holiday? But this is really like being afraid that a wife may become too beautiful, and I agree with Raymond Queneau – who for once was speaking in deadly earnest – that 'the people who whine about naughty robots and inhuman machinery have never proved anything except their own lack of imagination and fear of liberty'.

The greatest of the anxieties caused by science are certainly those concerned with its excess of power and with the heavy responsibility which results from that. One discovery alone, that of how to split the atom, has certainly placed the human race in a state of mortal – I was going to say sin! – danger. That great scientist Louis de Broglie has insisted on 'the almost tragic grandeur' of this state of affairs, which the Christian Berdiaeff prophesied as early as 1935 when he wrote: 'Technique may end in the extermination of the greater part of the human race and even in a cosmic catastrophe'.

The danger is not, perhaps, very worrying for the moment, but it may easily become more serious with the increase in the number of elements that can be disintegrated, and above all with the simplification of the apparatus required for producing fission. If we leave out of account the possibility of a premeditated act of destruction by war, which, whoever started it, would be the equivalent of a cross between murder and suicide, it is conceivable that planetary disaster might arise merely from some negligence in manipulation, or some mere inadvertence in the course of an experiment, or from some mistake in calculation – a mistake that is always possible, even with those impeccable machines upon which man will be more and more obliged to rely. Whether we like it or not, we are all of us now compelled to live our lives in a laboratory of atomic research, with all the insecurity which that involves: we are all of us condemned to some extent to 'live dangerously', as Nietzsche used to say, since our houses, though not perhaps built near Vesuvius, are situated on the same small globe as are the great atomic factories of the West and of the East.

Already, from time to time, there is talk of suspicious clouds, fogs and snows, or we are told that the earth is being surrounded by a radioactive layer, or that one of its poles is being weighed down. Such talk is, of course, inflated by the popular press, but what remains true is that a scientist never knows altogether what he is doing when he experiments. It is to this ignorance, indeed, that we owe the finest discoveries. How many great things have been discovered by surprise, or by chance! Röntgen did not know what he was doing when all of a sudden he saw the skeleton of his hand appear. The best we can hope is that the future will spare us an unexpected discovery that would blow up the earth.

Some people complain that we ought never to have gone so far: progress ought to have been stopped in time, the hellish road that led to the violation of the atom should have been barred. Wisdom after the event, and somewhat naïve at that. Could man stop midway? Could he forbid himself the exploration of certain territories? Could he stop dead in front of the post bearing the skull and crossbones and the word Danger?

Besides, the discovery of the splitting of the atom, though the most spectacular, is not the only one that places man in peril. There are also gases, microbes and viruses – to fill up the time while we wait for something more lethal. Is it proposed that, because of them, the laboratories should be closed and science sent to the Labour Exchange? Biology is a relatively harmless science, yet in wartime, or even in peacetime, it can lend its aid to unscrupulous governments that will not stop at any means of imposing their ideology and exterminating the adversary. There comes to mind the sterilisation applied by Hitler's régime, the means of sapping the mind used by totalitarian police, the intoxicants that produce confessions, etc. It is, alas, only too clear that everything that arms man can be turned against man, and that science – in so far as it is a dispenser of power – can render itself the innocent accomplice of fanaticism and despotism.

In addition to the dangers attaching to the criminal use of excessive power, science is bringing us a whole procession of other difficulties and embarrassments. To confine ourselves to biology, it is threatening – if that is the word – to extend the duration of old age to a point at which a nation would be in danger of sagging under the weight of its old people. And what will happen when someone has discovered the means of determining the sex of children? Will not the balance of the sexes soon be weighted in favour of boys? And are we going to welcome fatherless reproduction? Shall we allow the situation in which there would be two categories of human beings – those with two parents and those with only one? And what about test tube pregnancy? Or changes of sex in adult life?

A courageous jurist, Aurel David, has given vigorous expression to his horror at the violations of the organic person which result from grafting operations, and which are bound to increase in number with the advances of science. It is, in fact, he says, an important juridical innovation, a sort of moral revolution which has passed unnoticed, when 'certain parts of the body can be taken

E

from a corpse and applied to another person'. We have already mentioned the case of an individual whose intelligence was increased by the implantation of a gland from outside: is this individual, in whom an organ taken from somebody else is working and secreting, still strictly himself? And could he not say, like the poet: 'Je est un autre'? And what view are tradition and the law to take of this cavalier way of treating living fragments of the person as inanimate objects, as common things? of dividing man into spare parts and selling him by measure?

From this lowering, this 'chattelising' of the human body, Aurel David claims to draw the conclusion that the body must not be confused with the real person, which is, according to him, merely a small central nucleus, immutable, inalienable and similar in all individuals, the rest being nothing but 'a store of protoplasmic mechanisms, of extensions as foreign to the real person as are his furniture, his motor cars or his jewellery'.[1]

I cannot follow Aurel David in this curious speculation, or see in it any more than a desperate attempt to save the integrity of the human person and to set a barrier between it and the enterprises of technology. But at the same time we must be grateful to him for having forced us to pay attention to the incontestable fact that the very notion of 'person' is on the point of 'losing its naturalness'.

[1] See: Aurel David, *Vie et Pensée*, VIIe Congrès des Sociétés de philosophie de langue française, Grenoble, 13th-16th September 1954.

This naturalness of the person is menaced not only by the process of grafting: it can be foreseen that, in the near future, intellectual or moral merit will come under the control of a therapeutic art inspired by biology. Special hormones or other chemical agents will be used to reinforce the vigour of a man's mind, to strengthen his character, to dispose him to virtuousness. Quite soon, perhaps, people will buy genius or sanctity at the chemist's, just as women now buy the straightness of their nose or the depth of their gaze at the beauty parlour. The traditional notions of parenthood, maternity and sex are likewise in process of being *denatured*. '*Denatured Men*' . . . what a fine book for a future Vercors to write!

★

Which of all the promises of biology – so full of material for the enthusiasm of the scientist and the revue lyric writer – ought we to welcome, and which ought we to reject?

To what principle shall we appeal in deciding what is desirable, acceptable, legitimate? Upon what criterion shall we base choices that will commit the future? How shall we contrive to exercise the formidable powers allotted to us by science with a minimum of decency and dignity? How – without meeting the advantages offered by technology in a pusillanimous spirit of negation – shall we avoid finding ourselves on the perilous slope and yielding to the abuses of a Promethean intoxication?

It would be vain to claim to give a single overall solution to so many problems. Our task will be to improvise the solution for each one of them when the moment comes, taking account of the state of people's minds, of the collective mentality, of the social and moral situation. In this sort of thing there is no absolute rule, no dogmatic norm, no 'moral recipe' – as the philosopher Rauh put it, before the days of the doctrine of ambiguity. As each decision arises, we shall have to face the risk of miscalculation and mistaken action. We may have machines for thinking, but we shall never have machines for telling us our duty . . .

Rauh prophesied the arising of duties hitherto unknown, duties that would issue from science and might place us in situations of conflict: 'In general,' he said, 'it can be foreseen that the humanity to come will feel itself linked by duty to the well-being of the race. There will doubtless be sacrifices to the species, tragic situations in which sympathy and love will be found to be in conflict with *biological duty*.'

As for Carrel, he has this magnificent passage: 'For the first time since the beginning of its history, humanity has become master of its destiny . . . In order to grow afresh, it is forced to make itself anew. And it cannot make itself anew without pain, for it is both the marble and the sculptor. Out of its own substance it must send the splinters flying with great hammer-strokes, in order to recover its true face.'

★

Science has never yet had to repent of its contribution or to delete any of its advances. It has always maintained them and consolidated them, and has won the approval of public opinion even in cases where, at the beginning, this showed itself somewhat restive.[1] Never yet has science got into the position of having to turn back . . . And yet today, at certain moments, a slight doubt makes itself felt in us. We find ourselves wondering whether science is not on the point of reaching a kind of frontier, beyond which its progress might prove to be more harmful than advantageous. The feeling is one which it is rather difficult to justify, to provide with a logical basis: it is like an impression of uneasiness, a dull warning anxiety. May we not gradually, from one bold step to another, have entered certain fields which ought to have remained forbidden to us? Perhaps we ought not to have gone back to the sources of being? Perhaps human life should go on propagating itself in the shadow and science should never throw on it the beams of its intrusive light?

At the point we have reached, we already know too much not to be itching to go ahead with our adventure . . . Yet, however bold we may be – or think we are – however ready we may feel to devour without flinching all the fruits that have ripened on the tree of science, it must be admitted that something within us is anxious, is agitated and protests as it sees, outlined among the

---

[1] Let us recall the protests aroused by vaccination, by opo-therapy, and by anaesthesia. The use of ether and of chloroform in surgery was condemned by the physiologist Magendie in 1847 'in the name of morality and public security'.

mists of the future, the strange Paradise which the biologist is preparing for us. Yes, there is something in us that grudges its adherence to the organised, controlled, technicised, standardised, ascepticised world from which every spot has been bleached out and every element of chance, disorder or risk purged away. Are we quite sure that, by dint of progress, we shall not end by banishing something that makes us able to bear the old, imperfect world, that makes us find in it, in spite of everything, 'the heart to go on till evening'? Yes, certainly it will be the age of gold: born from selected seed, provided, every one of them, with faultless genes, and having had the benefit of super-active hormones and of a slight correction of the brain, all men will be handsome, healthy, strong and intelligent. People will live for two hundred years, or even more. There will be no more failure, no more fear, no more tragedy. Life will be safer, easier, longer, but will it still be worth living?

★

In the anxiety inspired in us by the giddy course of a science which, taken as a whole, threatens our globe with material destruction and is altering our spiritual climate, faced as we are by the encroachments of technical achievements which only a childish romantic can oppose and which our business is to master rather than to denigrate, all we can hope is that the scientist may consent to temper his boldness with scrupulousness, – that he will never forget that, according to Bacon's immortal phrase: 'Knowledge, if it be taken without the true corrective' – that of charity – 'hath in it some nature of venom or malignity.' And we must hope, above all, that agreement will be reached between all those who have both zest for the future and respect for humanity. As Canon Tiberghien has said: 'Moralists may have to pronounce upon these questions, but woe to the world if, when they are consulted, they cannot agree among themselves.'

This urgency of unanimity on the material issue is as great for biology as it is for nuclear physics.

What weight can divergencies of opinion have, or philosophical, theological, or ideological disagreements, when set against the community of those essential interests for which we are responsible? To spirit away, or to attenuate the dangers which are the price of our conquests, we shall need all the conscience that is available. The human race can only protect itself against itself by first becoming reconciled with itself.

III

CAN MAN BE MODIFIED?

CAN MAN BE MODIFIED? THE SUBJECT IS a vast one, and in order to go deeper we must at once set limits to it. Of course man can be changed: does he not receive some change, either physical or moral, from everything that happens to him – hygiene, exercise, sport, education, climate, politics, fashion . . .? We read a book or go to see a film, and we are no longer quite the same as before. Not to mention hair styles, make-up and plastic surgery, which gives 'beauty to the ugly'.

But, leaving all this aside, I intend to confine myself here to the modifications that might be made in the human being by the means provided by biology. And first of all I must insist on a point of major importance which is too often underrated – the fundamental stability of our species.

Contrary to popular belief, man has long since ceased to evolve. Present day man, the human being of the twentieth century, the human being that we are, does not differ essentially from the human being who lived in the caves of the Quaternary Age some 100,000 years ago, whose bony traces and rudimentary tools have been exhumed by the palaeontologists. The whole of that part of man's history which has gone by since those far-away ages has not, or has scarcely, altered the morphological and physiological outfit of our species. The enormous difference which none the less exists between the ancient flint-chipper and his modern heir is entirely the work of civilisation – that is to say, of the culture gradually accumulated and transmitted by social tradition. Already at the origin of the species man was equal to what he was destined to become. He carried within him, potentially, all the things that were destined gradually to expand and fructify in industry, in technical skill, in science, in art, in philosophy and in religion. So much so that if, by some miracle, it were possible to fetch a new born child of that past age into our own time and to bring him up and educate him as one of ours, he would become a man exactly like us: a man whom nothing, either in his appearance or in his conduct or in his private thoughts, would single out as a stranger among us, as a ghost from the past; a man who would meet with no particular difficulty in initiating himself into the complexities and refinements of our customs; a man who, finding himself on the same footing with the most advanced manifestations of thought or of aesthetics, would be able to argue about existentialism, or explain the painting of Picasso, as well as anybody else.

This certainly gives us the measure of the considerable importance which the social factor has in human evolution; but it must not make us forget that it was the *biological* factor that played the decisive part at the beginning of the adventure. That was the factor chiefly responsible for what, by analogy with the phrase 'the Greek miracle', might well be called 'the human miracle'. The fact that, starting from a certain moment in his history, and thanks to the combined play of intelligence and group instincts, man has been able to become what he now is, is due first and foremost to the occurrence of a small change – quite a small change – in his physical organism. To tell the truth, we do not know the exact nature and causes of this change, which was to produce *Homo sapiens* out of a primitive man who was not *sapiens*; but we do know that hardly had it established itself in human heredity before the great game had been implicitly played, – all the rest being merely the consequences and the working out. From that moment, because of that small alteration in his animal nature, man was bound to break for ever with the past. From the superior mammal which he was he became something quite different, – that 'unique being' who was to set so strong a mark upon the history of life, the history of the earth, and perhaps the history of the universe, and to inaugurate that prodigious adventure which, even today, is only in its first stage.

And certainly man is still far from having exhausted all his initial possibilities. But the problem now before us is whether these possibilities themselves could not be enlarged: whether this man which we are – which has not seriously changed its condition for about a thousand centuries and which, if subjected to the powers of nature only, seems destined not to evolve any more – could not, under its own steam, produce a fresh organic change in itself, a fresh bodily change with all the consequences to which such a change in animal nature might lead in the highest and most specifically human fields.

We shall not concern ourselves here with the question whether man has possibilities of becoming taller or more robust or more handsome, whether he can accentuate the shortening of his jaw to an extent that would rid him of his wisdom teeth, or whether he can complete the atrophy of his little toe . . . No, what interests, what fascinates us is the question whether he is likely to be able to increase the gap between him and primitive man, whether he can hope to make himself more intelligent, more clever, more sensitive, more disposed to solidarity and altruism, – in a word, more human.

Along these lines biology invites us to look forward: it suggests to us various dreams, which some people will call nightmares. These I will review, but not without the precaution of warning my readers that I do not necessarily approve of the use of all the procedures which science places at our service. When we are dealing with human affairs, emotional, moral and social conditions are added to the purely technical ones. We shall come back to this shortly: for the moment I will concentrate not on hopes but on facts.

*

It is obvious that this improvement which we contemplate making in the human being, this 'superhumanising' modification, must bear on the cerebral apparatus. Whatever opinion they may adopt about the nature of thought, people are agreed in admitting that the exceptional nature of the human psychical process is bound up with the structure and working of the brain. The brain is appreciably less voluminous in a large monkey than in *pithecanthropus*, in *pithecanthropus* than in primitive man, and in primitive man than in *Homo sapiens*. In addition structural differences have been noted, which have to do with the respective proportions of the lobes and with the complexity of the folds.

It would seem, *a priori*, easier to modify the function of the brain than its conformation. This functioning depends on chemical processes,[1] which we may hope to be able to influence favourably by means of appropriate substances. Students are already making use of stimulating or 'psychogenic' drugs, such as orthedrin and maxiton; glutamic acid is said to enable mice to find their way about more easily in a maze; it has been used in certain cases of mental backwardness.[2]

The most powerful of all the agents modifying vital phenomena are the hormones, and psychic activity

[1] The process of oxydation is slowed down in the brain tissue of certain 'idiots' (phenylpyruvic idiocy), who display disturbances of the metabolism, betrayed by an abnormal composition of the urine.

[2] J. B. S. Haldane has raised the question whether the presence of uric acid in the blood is not a normal stimulant of cerebral activity: it appears that patients suffering from hyperuricaemia (whose blood contains 80 milligrammes per litre instead of 40) are in a chronically doped state. (Ref. *Nature* 176, 1955).

does not escape their influence, for the brain, whatever else it is, is not an isolated organ. If there is a shortage of certain hormones in the blood medium – for example, of that secreted by the thyroid gland – the mental faculties burn low: they can be stimulated by artificially making up the quantity of the missing hormone. 'Thought', said Carrel, 'is the daughter of the internal secretions just as much as of the cerebral cortex. A man thinks, loves, suffers, admires and prays both with the whole of his brain and with all his organs.'

It could happen that one day we shall have available to us either natural or artificial hormones which, when administered to normal subjects, will have the effect of reinforcing their intellectual power. Just as at present a diabetic gives himself his insulin injection every morning to regulate the supply of sugar in the blood, so perhaps in the future everyone will give himself an injection of something or other to make him more intelligent.

Not only intelligence but character can be affected by chemical dosing. The male hormone (testosterone) makes people more virile, more courageous (it cures the capon of his 'caponishness'). Certain female hormones excite the maternal instinct. The future may bring the use of medicines that would favour social behaviour, kindness and devotion.[1]

Let us note in passing that the effect of diet has been considered from this point of view. 'Do we know the moral effect of food? Is there a philosophy of nutrition?'

---

[1] Carrel said that 'the Christian virtues' were 'harder to practise when our endocrine glands are deficient'.

wrote Nietzsche, in *The Joyful Wisdom*. Not to mention
Dr Laumonier who, in 1922, in his curious book
Thérapeutique des péchés capitaux, suggested curing
jealousy with milk, anger with fruit, pride with vege-
tables, vanity with laxatives and avarice with *nux
vomica*.

We are already in possession of extremely powerful
surgical methods for modifying affectivity – and it is
very difficult to draw the line between affectivity and
intelligence proper.[1] The cutting of a few nerve threads
may change a patient's personality, reduce a too strong
aggressiveness, put an end to intolerable fears. Although, for the present, operations of this kind (lobo-
tomy, etc.) are reserved for incurable cases, who with
their aid sometimes recover more or less normal
equilibrium, the possibility cannot be entirely excluded
that there may come into being a 'psychosurgery',
whose aim would be to raise the individual above
himself by obtaining the maximum output from his
affectivity.[2]

Let us pass now to the consideration of more radical
modifications of the brain – those which could be produced by operating on the embryo, whether this is

[1] Favourable modifications of affectivity can be obtained by
psychoanalytical treatment, but this aspect of the question is
outside our scope.

[2] Certain facts, which, to be sure, are exceptional and in-
sufficiently controlled, make one wonder whether skull injury
cannot be beneficent in effect on the intellectual faculties. In
Alfred de Vigny's *Journal d'un poète* we find this: 'Malebranche was
an idiot up to the age of seventeen. His head was injured in a fall,
he was trepanned, he became a man of genius.'

F

reached through the mother, or directly by means of a technique of ectogenesis.[1]

This ectogenesis – or 'test tube pregnancy' as it is more frivolously called – was depicted with great talent and humour by Aldous Huxley in his novel of the future, *Brave New World*.

Let us travel with him to the city of the future and penetrate into the Central Hatchery and Conditioning Centre, 'a squat grey building of only thirty-four stories'. Let us walk through the Fertilisation Room, casting a rapid glance at the stocks of sexual glands from which the germ cells of the coming generations will be drawn; then through the Bottling Room, then through the Organ Store, till we finally reach the Embryo Store, a huge dark room lit only by a red glow and with the stifling heat of a steamy bath. On the shelves thousands of fat jars extend as far as the eye can see, each of them containing a human embryo kept alive with artificial blood – a future citizen of the 'best of all possible worlds'. The jars move along automatically at the rate of 33·3 centimetres per hour, or 8 metres a day; by the end of 267 days, the normal period for the formation of the child, they have covered the 2,126 metres which they have to go to reach the Decanting Room, where at last the foetus will be taken out of its jar in the form of a new-born child. This has

[1] This is what Carrel had in mind when he wrote: 'One day some scientist will perhaps find the means of producing great men from ordinary children, as the bees transform a common larva into a queen bee by means of food which they have the art of preparing for it.'

rendered viviparous reproduction utterly out of date. For centuries now, humanity has ceased to procreate in the dirty and haphazard manner of the beasts. Having once and for all separated the pleasure of love from the duty of propagating the species, it has at the same time shaken off the burden of motherhood. The once sacred word 'mother' has become an impolite, grotesque word, hardly ever used, for it recalls the barbarous period when the human young were conceived blindly and born in pain and blood after having weighed down a woman's belly for nine months . . .

Is this Utopian? A mad dream? Not altogether. This vision of the future is based on a precise knowledge of the present. To be sure, we cannot, for the moment, cultivate human embryos in test tubes, but already we can keep the embryos of rats, mice, rabbits or guinea pigs alive for several days outside the womb; and the culture of embryos has indeed made considerable progress since Aldous Huxley wrote his *Brave New World*.[1] For it is now possible to construct, as it were, artificial organisms, complete with heart and lungs – it has been done by Carrel and Lindbergh, by Dr André-Thomas, and many others – whose characteristics approach nearer and nearer to the natural, both as regards the circulation of the blood or its equivalent, and as regards its oxygenation.

An intermediary solution of the problem of pregnancy is, indeed, conceivable: delivery could be stimu-

[1] Etienne Wolff has succeeded, with chickens, in cultivating most of the embryonic organs – bones, eyes, the syrinx, the sexual glands, etc. See Chapter I.

lated artificially and the embryo placed in culture at the age of two or three months: in short, a woman would reproduce like a kangaroo.

If ever partial or total 'test tube pregnancy' came to be applied to our species, various operations would become possible, resulting in a more or less profound modification of the human being in course of formation. It would then be no more than a game for the 'man-farming biologist' to change the subject's sex, the colour of its eyes, the general proportions of body and limbs, and perhaps the facial features.

Is it very rash to imagine that, in that case, it would be possible to increase the number of brain cells in the human member? A young embryo has already in its cerebral cortex the 9,000,000,000 pyramidal cells which will condition its mental activity during the whole of its life. This number, which is reached by geometrical progression or simple doubling, after thirty-three divisions of each cell (2, 4, 8, 16, 32 and so on), could in turn be doubled if we succeeded in causing just one more division – the thirty-fourth.[1]

It is true that some biologists are sceptical as to the possibility of such a huge enrichment of the brain: their view is that this organ has already reached a sort of structural ceiling, beyond which the species would no longer be viable.[2] Conklin predicts that 'the size of the

---

[1] One experimenter believes that he has increased the number of brain cells in the frog by submitting tadpoles to pituitary treatment.

[2] See C. Arambourg, *La Genèse de l'humanité*, Presses Universitaires Françaises, 1950.

head and that of the brain could not be much increased without making normal birth impossible and without destroying the harmonious correlation of the parts'.[1] The first of these objections would fall to the ground if science achieved ectogenesis and so reduced the delivery of a child to the emptying of a jar; and as for the second, it might well prove fallacious. If *pithecanthropus* had known anatomy, would not he too have thought he had reached the limit of brain size?

Finally, the brain, apart from its dimensions,[2] may present certain structural features related to the quality of its functioning. The left hemisphere predominates in right-handed people, the right hemisphere in left-handed, and some people believe that they have observed, in outstanding patients, a slightly more pronounced departure from symmetry than is normal between the two hemispheres. If this proves to be the case, it might be possible to accentuate this departure from symmetry by submitting the two cerebral hemispheres of the embryo to unequal conditions for growth.

★

The conclusion from these few indications is that biology may properly aim at helping the 'thinking reed' to think better. But it goes without saying that

[1] *Qu'est-ce que l'homme?*, 1941.

[2] It does not appear to be true that, when individuals are compared, the mass of the brain is correlated with intellectual power: see J. Lhermitte, *Le Cerveau et la Pensée*.

all the effects we have just envisaged, whether produced upon the human being when young, or upon the child, or upon the embryo, would still be limited to the individual thus modified. Let us assume that, by surgical or chemical means, we have succeeded in producing a better individual, a sort of 'superman'; this would still be no more than a somatic – the biological term is phenotypic – superhumanisation, with no effect on the potentialities of the germ cells. If this 'superman' were to procreate, even if he did so by union with a 'superwoman' obtained by the same methods, the two together would merely produce ordinary human beings, to whom the same superhumanising treatment would have to be applied, starting from the beginning. In fact, there is no transmission of characteristics acquired by the individual; or at any rate – I make this qualification deliberately, so as not to embark on polemics which would be outside the scope of this book – such transmission of acquired characteristics cannot be verified within the limits of experimental control.

Can we, then, not hope to modify a whole stock, not just human individuals, in order to create a race or species of human beings superior to that of the present day? Even though we do not know exactly what is responsible for the intellectual power of different individuals, and if we merely start from the very probable postulate that it depends in part on hereditary conditions,[1] it would be logical to try to reinforce it by

[1] I certainly do not mean to say that heredity is the *only* factor, or even that it is the principal factor, producing intellectual

using the method of *artificial selection*. This is a classic method, constantly used with success on plants and domestic animals. Every time it is proposed to accentuate this or that characteristic in a living stock, we choose as sires and dams the individuals that display this characteristic in the most marked degree, and by repeating the choice with every generation, we end by creating, more or less quickly, a stock that shows a notable improvement in the qualities in question. In this way we have created stocks of hens that lay more eggs or bigger eggs, stocks of cattle that yield more meat or more milk, stocks of sheep whose wool is longer or finer, stocks of horses that are faster, stocks of dogs that are easier to train, and so on. If it were possible to apply similar methods to our own species, we should have no difficulty in creating stocks of men who would be taller or shorter, stronger or weaker, handsomer or uglier, etc. When we come to the intellectual qualities the thing is less certain, but is still extremely probable.

This does not, of course, mean that better individuals will always produce better children, all that is assumed is that, *statistically*, the descendants of a large number of better individuals will be better than those of a large number of ordinary individuals. If each generation showed a slight rise in the intellectual level, this would be enough to produce an appreciable improvement at

superiority in human beings. The environmental conditions (family and social education, emotional shocks received in early childhood, etc.) without doubt play a large part in the formation of the psychic personality.

the end of twenty or thirty generations – that is to say, after several centuries.

This idea of *eugenic* selection of human beings is a very old one. In 548 B.C. Theognis of Megara wrote: 'One would not dream of buying cattle without thoroughly examining them, or a horse without knowing whether he came of a good stock; yet we see an excellent citizen being given to wife some wretched woman, daughter of a worthless father . . . Fortune mixes the races, and the odious adulteration is bastardising the species.' For already, among the Greeks, financial contingencies were upsetting the play of sexual selection!

A century later Plato, in the *Republic*, put into the mouth of Socrates a programme of eugenic marriage. The aim of an ideal city is to make 'marriages as healthy as possible, that is to say, as advantageous as they can be to the state, and to that end we must learn from the breeders of hunting dogs and birds of prey. What do they do, when they want to couple their beasts and obtain young? They single out from the herd the ones that excel the others. In the same way, if we want to prevent the human race from degenerating, we shall take care to encourage union between the better specimens of both sexes, and to limit that of the worse.'

In the seventeenth century Campanella, in the government of his 'City of the Sun', provided for a department which our age has not yet thought of – a Ministry of Love, whose business it would be to watch over marriage and procreation. And in 1801 the

French writer Robert le Jeune, in a strange pamphlet, revealed the secret of making great men whenever required. 'It is no more difficult', he asserts in his *Essai sur la mégalanthropogénésie*, 'to have intelligent children than to have an Arab horse, a short-legged basset hound or a pure-bred canary . . . Marry an intelligent man to an intelligent woman and you will get men of genius.' The idea is rather over-simplified, but in no way absurd. It was destined to be taken up again, in a more scientific spirit, by the anthropologist Vacher de Lapouge, who predicted that, if the function of reproduction were reserved to chosen individuals as an exclusive privilege, 'after a century or two, one would bump into men of genius in the street and the equivalents of our most illustrious scientists would be employed on road mending'. Lastly, the eminent American geneticist, H. J. Muller, winner of the Nobel Prize in 1946, has prophesied a rigorous selection limited to the male germ cell and consisting in a large increase in the descendants of great men through the use of modern techniques of artificial insemination.

To be sure, all this, with its slight odour of the 'human stud farm', may easily provoke a smile; and Georges Duhamel, who had little patience with 'scenes from the life of the future' in spite of his biological qualifications, did not fail to indulge in irony on the subject of the claims of positive eugenics.[1] 'Let us hope', he says, 'that the humanity of the future,

---

[1] The term is used in contradistinction to negative eugenics, which confines itself to trying to prevent propagation by individuals afflicted with grave hereditary defects.

governed by the new sciences, will engender as many outstanding men as it has produced hitherto at random and in ignorance.'

For my part, I think this sort of ridicule is out of place. There seems hardly any doubt that, under a system of artificial selection, the proportion of human beings of high quality would be bound to become greater – and, indeed, much greater – than it is in our time. It is even probable that there would arise individuals whose spiritual calibre would surpass anything that humanity has so far known. Until human selection has been tried, nobody has the right to assign an upper limit to man. That does not, indeed, mean that such selection ought to be put into practice. But at least it is essential to recognise honestly what advantages it might bring to mankind, and to know, if we reject it, what we are rejecting with it.

Besides, human selection is, theoretically, not the only method of improving our species available to biology. Already we know, in the case of a large number of living creatures of various kinds, how to produce hereditary changes, *mutations*, by means of artificial agents, and in particular by means of low-wavelength radiations, such as X-rays, or the gamma rays, or radium, and also by certain chemical substances such as yperite, the sulfamides and phenol. In this way it is easy to create new races of living things. But, on the one hand, these artificial stocks are nearly always, not to say always, inferior to the normal type of the species; and, on the other hand, we are incapable of producing this or that modification at will.

All that we know, when we are employing one of these 'mutagenic' treatments, is that we shall see new forms appear among the descendants of the subjects treated, without our being able to predict what their novelty will consist in. It is obvious that, in these circumstances, no one would dream of applying one of these 'mutagenic' treatments to the human species.

Let us add that, in certain microbes, and still only in exceptional cases, it is possible to produce *precise* hereditary changes – controlled mutations – by the use of chemical substances which can modify heredity. There is no reason not to suppose that, in the future, we shall learn how to make human hereditary characteristics mutate in a direction that will be both predictable and advantageous. When that day comes, man will be able to modify himself when and how he wishes. But in any case the realisation of this ambitious hope appears to be a long way off, having regard to the number of tentative experiments that would certainly be necessary in order to perfect a suitable technique.

★

Mention must lastly be made of a very special kind of mutation which can already be produced at will – an increase in the number of sets of chromosomes. In every organism born of two parents, the chromosomes – which are, as is well known, the principal artisans of heredity – form two sets, one of which comes from the mother, and the other from the father. In plants it is possible, by chemical means, to cause quite easily the doubling of these sets, so that there are then four of them. The plants obtained in this way are definitely larger than their relatives with only two sets; they are also more vigorous and more resistant to cold and drought. Turning to animals, we have not yet found out how to produce similar stocks with four sets of chromosomes, but salamanders, frogs and even, so it seems, mice and rabbits with three sets have been brought into existence – animals, that is to say, which contain two maternal sets and one paternal, and are therefore twice children of their mother and only once of their father. The salamanders and frogs with three sets of chromosomes are not bigger or more robust than the normal specimens of the same species; but, according to the Swedish experimenters, Häggqvist and Bane, rabbits with three sets appear to be abnormally large and precocious. One cannot help wondering whether men with three or four sets of chromosomes would be viable and whether, supposing they were, they would display any advantageous characteristics in comparison with human beings with two sets. Any attempt at prediction on this subject would be premature: let us merely say that, if such chromosomic mutation seemed likely to be profitable to the human species, we should not come up against any very great practical difficulties in obtaining it.

*

That is a very brief outline, as objective as possible,

of the way in which the problem of the modification of man by biological means presents itself to our view, if we leave out all emotional, social or moral objections and considering our species, deliberately, as a mere animal species, to be improved at our convenience. It shows plainly that the idea of a creature superior to man emerges quite naturally from the facts. It had, indeed, preceded them, for the myth of the 'superman' was invented by philosophers before it found a rational basis in science. I think it is in Act One of Goethe's *Faust* that the word superman, 'Übermensch', appears for the first time, when the Spirit rises before the terrified gaze of the old Doctor and says:

> Now I am here. What a sad shuddering
> Seizes the Superman.

We all know what fame – also what harm – Nietzsche brought to the idea of Superman: ever since *Zarathustra* an odour of inhuman aristocratism has clung to it, and this inevitably renders it suspect to many people. 'Man', said Nietzsche, 'is something that has to be surmounted . . . What is a monkey to a man? An object of ridicule or of painful shame. And that is what man must be to superman: an object of ridicule and of painful shame.' And again: 'Man is a rope stretched between the animal and the superhuman, a rope across the abyss . . . Formerly they said God, now I have taught you to say Superman.' To the great solitary of Sils Maria the question presented itself, indeed, as a spiritual rather than a bodily 'superhumanisation', to be realised in a *transmutation* – a deChristianisation – of all moral values.

In contrast, it was definitely a *biological superman* that Renan had in mind when he wrote in his *Dialogues* (1871): 'A far-reaching application of physiology and of the principle of selection might lead to the creation of a superior race, whose right to govern would reside not only in its science, but in the very superiority of its blood, its brain, its nervous system.' According to this conception of Renan's, Superman would have domination over man as we today have over the animals, but there would be joy in submitting to him, for he would be – or at least we may hope so – an incarnation of the divine.

Edgar Quinet's vision of the future is more gloomy. Overwhelmed by the revelations of the first 'transformists', he went so far as to predict the decline of man, supplanted by a triumphant heir. In an admirable passage of his book, *La Création*, Quinet writes: 'Man knew that he was not immortal, but until that moment he had convinced himself that, if he should perish, everything that has life would perish with him. He imagined that he had so thoroughly taken possession of the earth, that it could now belong only to him. The idea of having successors had never entered his head. Without him there would be no life, no progress any more, only an empty and desolate, orphaned world, in perpetual mourning for vanished man: the globe would have become a sepulchre . . . But now we must accustom ourselves to the news that man will pass . . . And that is a prophecy that surpasses all the prophecies of

Isaiah and Ezekiel.' This creature which will succeed us will admire some of our productions – he will respect our geometry, but 'perhaps in the same way as we admire and respect the bee's hexagons and the bird's nests. "What a fine coral reef!" he will say, and will mean the Parthenon. "What exquisite bird song!" and it will be the *Iliad*.' What will become of man when he is thus surpassed? Will he let himself be herded back into the woods and the islands, as we, at this moment, have herded back the bison and the ibex? Quinet thinks he will not: for man 'is not one of those kings who survive their dethronement.' If, all of a sudden, 'rounding some corner of a rocky gorge, he found that his absolute royalty was disputed and that he had met his master, he would rush from the stage rather than accept the secondary part; he would perish rather than become his successor's pet or cattle.'

Biology, as we have just seen, gives a new actuality to this eloquent text, although the problem does not confront us exactly as it confronted Edgar Quinet. To us the problem is not whether to offer resistance to a more gifted successor brought into being by the natural play of organic evolution, but whether we ourselves, by our own means, will be able and willing to draw out of ourselves a being that will excel us.

Is the creation of such a superman desirable? And shall we, to achieve it, consent to use the resources which science is obtaining for us? This is the point we must now deal with, and it is one that touches upon the gravest difficulties we have yet encountered, for the question of Superman is only one aspect of a far wider question, – that of man laying hands upon himself, of the application of biological techniques to the human person.

Up to now, biology has scarcely impinged upon our lives, except through the intermediary of its daughter, medicine; but it will not always be able to keep up this discretion. It has reached a point of maturity at which its discoveries and inventions have more or less powerful repercussions upon the fate of individuals or of the species. It is no accident that, not long ago, Father Riquet preached a series of Lenten sermons in Notre-Dame on the Gospels and Biology. Nor that, at Montpellier, the thirty-eighth *Semaine sociale de France* took as its subject the consideration of the social and human consequences of the progress of biology. In the course of this cycle of lectures and classes, various eminent speakers of undeniable qualifications – among others Professor Rémy Collin – one after another examined, from the Catholic point of view, the problems of artifical insemination, voluntary sex determination, eugenics, parthenogenesis (or fatherless reproduction), artificial mutation, selection and even superhumanisation, which – as Canon Tiberghien put it – it is impossible to view without a feeling of dizziness.

Scientists, moralists and priests all uttered cries of alarm in face of the possibilities already open to mankind in the field of dominated, controlled and directed reproduction. They gave various warnings of the danger – as they saw it – of letting loose a kind of science-mania, a Promethean or even Lucifier-like enthusiasm proceeding directly, in their view, from 'atheistic humanism'; they tried to put scientists on their guard against the perilous feeling of omnipotence which tempts the creature to play the Creator; they affirmed the necessity of keeping the human person out of reach of degrading or dangerous experiments 'which smack of the veterinary surgeon's consulting room or of the research laboratory' (Collin), in which they saw a fresh episode in the battle of 'man against the human'.

There is certainly some foundation for such uneasiness, and it is no bad thing that men who have a high and sacred idea of man, because they see in the human a reflection of the divine, should give voice to the protest of the spirit and the heart against the encroachments of a science which, to use the words of Valéry's Faust, 'is gropingly beginning to touch the sources of life'. Indeed, the fact that one admires the marvellous advances of biology and cannot help feeling some enthusiasm at the magnificent prospects which the laboratory lays open for the future of mankind, is no reason for not seeing, not understanding, not feeling the causes for anxiety there are in the spectacle of man gradually, with his clumsy hands, approaching mankind and proposing to submit it to the results of a still faltering witchcraft. Our joy and pride are far from being unmixed. What biologist worthy of the name could, even if he had tried to bring it about, watch without a secret fear the approach of the hour when technique will dare to lay its hands on the thinking being? We who are called 'scientists' – and it is a name

G

we do not refuse, for there are less honourable ones –
are not as grossly and naïvely insensitive as people are
apt to believe. The fact that we persist in regarding
man as part of nature does not make us have less respect for him or incline us to treat him without ceremony.
I will even go so far as to say that perhaps respect for
mankind should be even greater in those who believe
only in man, – in those who, stripped of every illusion
about transcendence, can only see in man an animal
unlike any other, with no obligation except towards
itself, with no law to obey except its own and with no
values to revere except those of its own making.

However man looks at himself, and whether he likes
it or not – whether he believes in it or not – he cannot
help regarding himself as something sacred. He cannot
help regarding himself as the highest and most precious
thing on the planet, the culmination of a slow and
laborious evolution of which he is far from having
understood all the detailed workings, as that 'unique
being' which can never be remade or replaced, and
which perhaps has not its like in the whole of the vast
universe: a miracle of chance, or of some nameless and
unnameable agency, – but still a miracle . . . What a
responsibility, to lay hands on that! . . . But will it be
any less a responsibility if, by resolutely taking the side
of inaction, of non-intervention, we deprive man of the
improvements in his nature which he could gain from
a judicious application of science? Our inertia and
passivity commit us no less than our zeal, our acts of
refusal no less than our acts of consent: they all help to
make man what he is – that is to say (as it seems to

those who admit they do not know what man is), to fashion a mystery and to build the unknown.

Part of my idea of man is my feeling of his boldness, of his determination to rise higher and become more. For this reason I shall not say, as many do, that man is good enough as he is. I shall not say: 'What is the use of our making a superman, when man is already big enough to endanger his existence?' I shall not say: 'What is the good of giving man more intelligence? It will not make him any happier.' I shall not say that a society of geniuses would be incapable of going on existing – for genius is a relative thing, and, compared to Neanderthal man, our species was already, at its start, a collection of geniuses. Nor shall I say that the creation of a superman would amount to the suicide of our own humanity, – for there are perhaps, in man, values he ought to prefer even to his own existence. I shall take it as a postulate that man must aim at surpassing himself, at drawing from himself something better than himself.

But, however legitimate and magnificent such a dream may seem to us, one is none the less fully conscious of the formidable difficulties that are raised by the idea of an evolution controlled and directed by man.

The better to separate ourselves from the animal, shall we consent to use upon ourselves techniques that have hitherto been confined to animals? If, as Pascal said, the whole problem of morality is to '*travailler à bien penser*', shall we consent, sometimes, to come into collision with morality in order to stimulate the progress of intelligence? And – most important of all – at what kind of superman will it be right to aim? In what direction are we to steer evolutionary progress? What should be our ideal of the individual and society? Agreement might be easily reached on the criteria of intellectual superiority, but to what can we appeal in order to establish those of moral superiority?

It is here that the adversaries of science – and there are many of these ungrateful people, who abuse science while they profit greedily from its benefits – believe that they are on good ground, when they reproach it for leaving us with our souls defenceless against the power which it confers on us.

Let us first point out that science would have a perfect right to adopt such an attitude – the amoralist attitude. Science does not, as science, set up to be a sovereign guide, a dictator of conduct. It does not claim to be a unique or supreme value; for we have recovered from the naïve illusions that were current in the nineteenth century, and we no longer say, like Renan and Berthelot, that science must take the place of everything that is not science. To be sure, science, as the maker of truth, is in our view sacred, but at the same time we do not think it the only thing that is sacred. Being amoral by its very nature and purpose and, to use Henri Poincarè's celebrated phrase, 'speaking in the indicative and not in the imperative', it will do its job as science and will leave to non-science the business of enlightening men's consciences. It will entrust to non-science the guardianship of the necessary values and will ask to be confined within proper limits and to be warned against its own abuses. This 'non-science' will be – as the case may be – some form of mysticism, some ideology, or a kind of humanism . . .

That is the classic doctrine of the fundamentally amoral nature of science. There is a good deal of truth in it. And yet, although perhaps science has not much to say about morality, I consider that it cannot remain *wholly silent* and that the few words it might be able to contribute would have special weight.

Many people have tried to extract these few words from biology. Virtue, said Carrel, is to avoid the sin against nature: it is to keep healthy and manly, to respect life in oneself and in others, to try to propagate it in the best possible conditions, to protect the integrity of one's physical being against undermining or intoxicants, and that of one's moral being against falsehood, futility and calumny . . .

For my part, without contesting the value of a biological decalogue *à la* Carrel,[1] I believe that those who cherish the hope of establishing a sort of treaty between science and conscience must turn, rather, towards another science – the science of mind, and in particular psychoanalysis.

Psychoanalysis, in fact, reveals to us the fundamental part played by feeling, by affectivity, in human conduct.

[1] In a small and remarkable book (*Physiologie des moeurs*, Presses Universitaires Françaises, 1953), Dr Paul Chauchard has attempted in his turn, to base a system of morality upon positive knowledge, and in particular upon the data supplied by biology.

It teaches us how this emotional equipment evolves during the course of the individual life, and by what subtle alchemy primitive egoism is transmuted into love of one's neighbour or attachment to an ideal. It makes us conscious of the rich humus of the soul, into which what Kant calls the 'noble stem of duty' plunges for its enrichment.

Now that we have learnt from psychoanalysis what is contained in the human heart – which, as Simone Weil said, is 'just as much a natural reality as is the trajectory of a star' – we no longer have the right to think of morality as simply a 'predisposition to the good'. We know that the man who is egotistical, greedy and selfish, far from representing a superior type of human being, is merely a case of arrested development, a man who has failed to attain spiritual maturity, an emotionally backward person, instinctually infantile – *a kind of subman*. The lack of the capacity to love one's neighbour – or at any rate to love something other than oneself – is a deficiency, a weakness if not a sickness. There is only one way for a human being to rise, to grow, to become 'more of a man' in Vercors' phrase, and that is through generosity, devotion, the giving of oneself.

And so, by the round-about way of psychoanalysis, we come back to that lofty 'scientific morality' which was outlined at the beginning of the century by the philosopher Guyau when he showed how duty was bound up with the organic instincts of vitality, fertility and love. We have moved a long way since the time – the time of my childhood – when that beloved and honest man Le Dantec preached, in red covered books which the worst bands of hooligans exploited as their justification, that egoism is the 'one and only basis of all society,' and refused to see in the social tendencies of mankind any more than 'the traces left by deformations caused by living in common'. Nowadays we should be more inclined to say that love is the one and only basis of all society . . .[1]

And let us not forget that this human love, which science recognises as an essential attribute of the species and indicates to us as the basis of a natural morality, this love on whose account we ought never to despair of mankind however alarming its future may look, was constantly necessary, and still is, to the advance of science itself. For if there had been nothing but cold logic and insensitive reason, science would never have come into existence. One might even, with a slight flamboyance, go so far as to say that there is no science entirely devoid of conscience, for there is no science without love. By what would the scientist be carried forward and upheld, if not by the strange 'passion for knowledge'? 'In spite of their defects and their vices,' said Charles Richet, 'scientists have all of them the same soul; for all have the worship of truth for its own sake; they are all moved by one thought in common: the love of the truth hidden in things.'

---

[1] 'In the development of mankind as a whole, just as in individuals, love alone acts as the civilising factor in the sense that it brings a change from egoism to altruism.' (Sigmund Freud, *Group Psychology and the Analysis of the Ego*, translated by James Strachey, International Psycho-analytical Library, no. 6, p. 57.)

'The worship of truth for its own sake . . .' Yes, these men in love with truth are not thinking of the consequences, of the possible applications of what they may discover – or, if they do think of them, it is merely because these things confirm that they are in touch with the real. What they desire – the one thing that in their eyes can, in the words of Ramon y Cajal, 'justify living' – is simply to reach 'that which is'. Truth is something they love for its own sake, in a way that is imperious, irrational, unyielding and unrelenting. They love it as one always loves – because they are they and it is it. They love it so much that they find honour, and almost find delight, in proclaiming when it goes against them. And this is why they will not admit or endure that anyone, for the sake of any motive, cause or ideal, however lofty it may seem, should denature the truth or even add to it. They serve truth with an unscrupulous devotion, convinced that it is impossible ever to go too far in zeal for it, and content to devote to its service the passion, the worship, the fury which, everywhere else, is its enemy. They know that truth is arduous and fragile – that, like Chekhov's God, we are in danger of losing it the moment we believe we have hold of it. They know that no one can get near it without having overcome himself – that, as Leonardo said, it is never where men shout, and scarcely ever where they speak.

Love of *that which is, simply because it is.* Love, not mere curiosity, – even though Simone Weil would like to deny us the right to love scientific truth on the ground that it contains no good for the heart of man.

No good? To begin with, that is not certain. The

greatest scientist of all, Einstein, bowed down with religious fervour before the supremely rational harmony of the laws of nature. Others, it is true, prefer to ascribe no characteristics to 'that which is', since any qualification appears to them a limitation and almost a blasphemy. For they consider that 'that which is' goes beyond all human language, and that there is more meaning, more grandeur and poetry in that small verb than in the most majestic epithets. In this, indeed, they are at one with a poet, for was it not the enchanting Katherine Mansfield who said: 'At the end *truth* is the only thing *worth having*: it's more thrilling than love, more joyful and more passionate.'